Travels with a Donkey

in the

Cevennes

by

Robert Louis Stevenson

With Advice for Modern Travellers
following in the Footsteps and Hoofprints of
the Original Adventurers –
by
Laurence Phillips

im/rint

www.imprintillyria.com

Aknowledgements

Laurence Phillips would like to thank the Association Sur le Chemin de RL Stevenson for their kind assistance and for the map on page 143. And a very special thanks to Brigitte Donnadieu for sharing her infectious delight in such a magical corner of the world – surely the best kept secret in France.

Published by Imprint Illyria Books

Travels with a Donkey in the Cevennes first published 1879
In the Footsteps of RLS © copyright Laurence Phillips 2009
This edition © imprint illyria books 2009

This edition first published 2009

ISBN 978-0-9558247-3-9

Cover design © imprint illyria 2009
Printed and bound by CPI Antony Rowe, Eastbourne

imprint illyria books
London

CONTENTS

Travels With a Donkey in The Cevennes

In the Footsteps of RLS   by Laurence Phillips

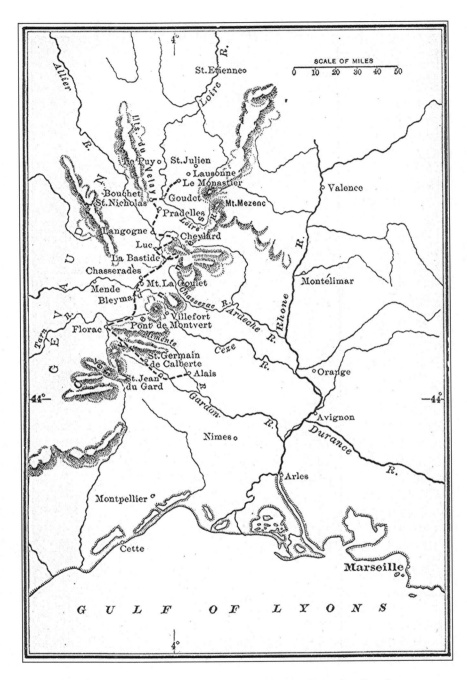

1878 Map of Stevenson's original Travels with a Donkey

Dear Sidney Colvin,

The journey which this little book is to describe was very agreeable and fortunate for me. After an uncouth beginning, I had the best of luck to the end. But we are all travellers in what John Bunyan calls the wilderness of this world - all, too, travellers with a donkey: and the best that we find in our travels is an honest friend. He is a fortunate voyager who finds many. We travel, indeed, to find them. They are the end and the reward of life. They keep us worthy of ourselves; and when we are alone, we are only nearer to the absent.

Every book is, in an intimate sense, a circular letter to the friends of him who writes it. They alone take his meaning; they find private messages, assurances of love, and expressions of gratitude, dropped for them in every corner. The public is but a generous patron who defrays the postage. Yet though the letter is directed to all, we have an old and kindly custom of addressing it on the outside to one. Of what shall a man be proud, if he is not proud of his friends?

And so, my dear Sidney Colvin, it is with pride that I sign myself affectionately yours,

R. L. S.

Robert Louis Stevenson (1850-94) is best known as the Scottish author of Treasure Island (1883) The Strange Case of Dr Jekyll and Mr Hyde (1886) and A Child's Garden of Verses (1885). In 1879, he published Travels with a Donkey in the Cevennes, his account of a 12-day September hike in 1878 through the heart of France. Stevenson undertook the journey as much to explore the raw countryside shaped by nature, history and the passions of religion, as to forget the heartache the return of his beloved Fanny Osbourne to her native United States. Years later, Fanny & Robert were to be re-united andeventually married. Stevenson's Cevennes journey inspired the GR70 national footpath.

5

Velay

Many are the mighty things, and nought is more mighty than man. . . .
He masters by his devices the tenant of the fields.

SOPHOCLES.

Who hath loosed the bands of the wild ass?

JOB.

Chapter One

The donkey,
the pack &
the pack-saddle

IN A LITTLE PLACE called Le Monastier, in a pleasant highland valley fifteen miles from Le Puy, I spent about a month of fine days. Monastier is notable for the making of lace, for drunkenness, for freedom of language, and for unparalleled political dissension. There are adherents of each of the four French parties - Legitimists, Orleanists, Imperialists, and Republicans - in this little mountain-town; and they all hate, loathe, decry, and calumniate each other. Except for business purposes, or to give each other the lie in a tavern brawl, they have laid aside even the civility of speech. 'Tis a mere mountain Poland.

In the midst of this Babylon I found myself a rallying-point; every one was anxious to be kind and helpful to the stranger. This was not merely from the natural hospitality of mountain people, nor even from the surprise with which I was regarded as a man living of his own free will in Le Monastier, when he might just as well have lived anywhere else in this big world; it arose a good deal from my projected excursion southward through the Cevennes. A traveller of my sort was a thing hitherto unheard of in that district. I was looked upon with contempt, like a man who should project a journey to the moon, but yet with a respectful interest, like one setting forth for the inclement

Pole. All were ready to help in my preparations; a crowd of sympathisers supported me at the critical moment of a bargain; not a step was taken but was heralded by glasses round and celebrated by a dinner or a breakfast.

It was already hard upon October before I was ready to set forth, and at the high altitudes over which my road lay there was no Indian summer to be looked for. I was determined, if not to camp out, at least to have the means of camping out in my possession; for there is nothing more harassing to an easy mind than the necessity of reaching shelter by dusk, and the hospitality of a village inn is not always to be reckoned sure by those who trudge on foot. A tent, above all for a solitary traveller, is troublesome to pitch, and troublesome to strike again; and even on the march it forms a conspicuous feature in your baggage. A sleeping-sack, on the other hand, is always ready - you have only to get into it; it serves a double purpose - a bed by night, a portmanteau by day; and it does not advertise your intention of camping out to every curious passer-by. This is a huge point. If a camp is not secret, it is but a troubled resting-place; you become a public character; the convivial rustic visits your bedside after an early supper; and you must sleep with one eye open, and be up before the day. I decided on a sleeping-sack; and after repeated visits to Le Puy, and a deal of high living for myself and my advisers, a sleeping-sack was designed, constructed, and triumphantly brought home.

This child of my invention was nearly six feet square, exclusive of two triangular flaps to serve as a pillow by night and as the top and bottom of the sack by day. I call it 'the sack,' but it was never a sack by more than courtesy: only a sort of long roll or sausage, green waterproof cart-cloth without and blue sheep's fur within. It was commodious as a valise, warm and dry for a bed. There was luxurious turning room for one; and at a pinch the thing might serve for two. I could bury myself in it up to the neck; for my head I trusted to a fur cap, with a hood to fold down over my ears and a band to pass under my nose like a respirator; and in case of heavy rain I proposed to make myself a little tent, or tentlet, with my waterproof coat, three stones, and a bent branch.

It will readily be conceived that I could not carry this huge package on my own, merely human, shoulders. It remained to choose a beast of burden. Now, a horse is a fine lady among animals, flighty, timid, delicate in eating, of tender health; he is too valuable and too restive to be left alone, so that you are chained to your brute as to a fellow galley-slave; a dangerous road puts him out of his wits; in short, he's an uncertain and exacting ally, and adds thirty-fold to the troubles of the voyager. What I

8

required was something cheap and small and hardy, and of a stolid and peaceful temper; and all these requisites pointed to a donkey.

There dwelt an old man in Monastier, of rather unsound intellect according to some, much followed by street-boys, and known to fame as Father Adam. Father Adam had a cart, and to draw the cart a diminutive she-ass, not much bigger than a dog, the colour of a mouse, with a kindly eye and a determined under-jaw. There was something neat and high-bred, a quakerish elegance, about the rogue that hit my fancy on the spot. Our first interview was in Monastier market-place. To prove her good temper, one child after another was set upon her back to ride, and one after another went head over heels into the air; until a want of confidence began to reign in youthful bosoms, and the experiment was discontinued from a dearth of subjects. I was already backed by a deputation of my friends; but as if this were not enough, all the buyers and sellers came round and helped me in the bargain; and the ass and I and Father Adam were the centre of a hubbub for near half an hour. At length she passed into my service for the consideration of sixty-five francs and a glass of brandy. The sack had already cost eighty francs and two glasses of beer; so that Modestine, as I instantly baptized her, was upon all accounts the cheaper article. Indeed, that was as it should be; for she was only an appurtenance of my mattress, or self-acting bedstead on four castors.

I had a last interview with Father Adam in a billiard-room at the witching hour of dawn, when I administered the brandy. He professed himself greatly touched by the separation, and declared he had often bought white bread for the donkey when he had been content with black bread for himself; but this, according to the best authorities, must have been a flight of fancy. He had a name in the village for brutally misusing the ass; yet it is certain that he shed a tear, and the tear made a clean mark down one cheek.

By the advice of a fallacious local saddler, a leather pad was made for me with rings to fasten on my bundle; and I thoughtfully completed my kit and arranged my toilette. By way of armoury and utensils, I took a revolver, a little spirit-lamp and pan, a lantern and some halfpenny candles, a jack-knife and a large leather flask. The main cargo consisted of two entire changes of warm clothing - besides my travelling wear of country velveteen, pilot-coat, and knitted spencer - some books, and my railway-rug, which, being also in the form of a bag, made me a double castle for cold nights. The permanent larder was represented by cakes of chocolate and tins of Bologna sausage. All this, except what I carried about my person, was easily stowed into the sheepskin bag; and by good fortune I threw in my empty knapsack, rather for convenience of carriage than from any thought that I should want it on my journey. For more immediate needs I took a leg of cold mutton, a bottle of Beaujolais, an empty bottle to carry milk, an egg-beater, and a considerable quantity of black bread and white, like Father Adam, for myself and donkey, only in my scheme of things the destinations were reversed.

Monastrians, of all shades of thought in politics, had agreed in threatening me with many ludicrous misadventures, and with sudden death in many surprising forms. Cold, wolves, robbers, above all the nocturnal practical joker, were daily and eloquently forced on my attention. Yet in these vaticinations, the true, patent danger was left out. Like Christian, it was from my pack I suffered by the way. Before telling my own mishaps, let me in two words relate the lesson of my experience. If the pack is well strapped at the ends, and hung at full length—not doubled, for your life - across the pack-saddle, the traveller is safe. The saddle will certainly not fit, such is the imperfection of our transitory life; it will assuredly topple and tend to overset; but there are stones on every roadside, and a man soon learns the art of correcting any tendency to overbalance with a well-adjusted stone.

On the day of my departure I was up a little after five; by six, we began to load the donkey; and ten minutes after, my hopes were in the dust. The pad would not stay on Modestine's back for half a moment. I returned it to its maker, with whom I had so contumelious a passage that the street outside was crowded from wall to wall with gossips looking on and listening. The pad changed hands with much vivacity; perhaps it would be more descriptive to say that we threw it at each other's heads; and, at any rate, we were very warm and unfriendly, and spoke with a deal of freedom.

I had a common donkey pack-saddle - a barde, as they call it - fitted upon Modestine; and once more loaded her with my effects. The doubled sack, my pilot-coat (for it was warm, and I was to walk in my waistcoat), a great bar of black bread, and an open basket containing the white bread, the mutton, and the bottles, were all corded together in a very elaborate system of knots, and I looked on the result with fatuous content. In such a monstrous deck-cargo, all poised above the donkey's shoulders, with nothing below to balance, on a brand-new pack-saddle that had not yet been worn to fit the animal, and fastened with brand-new girths that might be expected to stretch and slacken by the way, even a very careless traveller should have seen disaster brewing. That elaborate system of knots, again, was the work of too many sympathisers to be very artfully designed. It is true they tightened the cords with a will; as many as three at a time would have a foot against Modestine's quarters, and be hauling with clenched teeth; but I learned afterwards that one thoughtful person, without any exercise of force, can make a more solid job than half-a-dozen heated and enthusiastic grooms.

I was then but a novice; even after the misadventure of the pad nothing could disturb my security, and I went forth from the stable door as an ox goeth to the slaughter.

Father Adam demonstrates Modestine's docile nature
(After Edouardo Zamacois y Zabala's "Taming the Donkey")

Chapter Two

The green donkey-driver

T HE BELL OF MONASTIER was just striking nine as I got quit of these preliminary troubles and descended the hill through the common. As long as I was within sight of the windows, a secret shame and the fear of some laughable defeat withheld me from tampering with Modestine. She tripped along upon her four small hoofs with a sober daintiness of gait; from time to time she shook her ears or her tail; and she looked so small under the bundle that my mind misgave me. We got across the ford without difficulty - there was no doubt about the matter, she was docility itself - and once on the other bank, where the road begins to mount through pine-woods, I took in my right hand the unhallowed staff, and with a quaking spirit applied it to the donkey. Modestine brisked up her pace for perhaps three steps, and then relapsed into her former minuet.

Another application had the same effect, and so with the third. I am worthy the name of an Englishman, and it goes against my conscience to lay my hand rudely on a female. I desisted, and looked her all over from head to foot; the poor brute's knees were trembling and her breathing was distressed; it was plain that she could go no faster on a hill. God forbid, thought I, that I should brutalise this innocent creature; let her go at her own pace, and let me patiently follow.

What that pace was, there is no word mean enough to describe; it was something as much slower than a walk as a walk is slower than a run; it kept me hanging on each foot for an incredible length of time; in five minutes it exhausted the spirit and set up a fever in all the muscles of the leg. And yet I had to keep close at hand and measure my advance exactly upon hers; for if I dropped a few yards into the rear, or went on a few yards ahead, Modestine came instantly to a halt and began to browse. The thought that this was to last from here to Alais nearly broke my heart. Of all conceivable journeys, this promised to be the most tedious. I tried to tell myself it was a lovely day; I tried to charm my foreboding spirit with tobacco; but I had a vision ever present to me of the long, long roads, up hill and down dale, and a pair of figures ever infinitesimally moving, foot by foot, a yard to the minute, and, like things enchanted in a nightmare, approaching no nearer to the goal.

In the meantime there came up behind us a tall peasant, perhaps forty years of age, of an ironical snuffy countenance, and arrayed in the green tail-coat of the country. He overtook us hand over hand, and stopped to consider our pitiful advance.

'Your donkey,' says he, 'is very old?'

I told him, I believed not.

Then, he supposed, we had come far.

I told him, we had but newly left Monastier.

'Et vous marchez comme ca!' cried he; and, throwing back his head, he laughed long and heartily. I watched him, half prepared to feel offended, until he had satisfied his mirth; and then, 'You must have no pity on these animals,' said he; and, plucking a switch out of a thicket, he began to lace Modestine about the stern-works, uttering a cry. The rogue pricked up her ears and broke into a good round pace, which she kept up without flagging, and without exhibiting the least symptom of distress, as long as the peasant kept beside us. Her former panting and shaking had been, I regret to say, a piece of comedy.

My deus ex machina, before he left me, supplied some excellent, if inhumane, advice; presented me with the switch, which he declared she would feel more tenderly than my cane; and finally taught me the true cry or masonic word of donkey-drivers, 'Proot!' All the time, he regarded me

14

with a comical, incredulous air, which was embarrassing to confront; and smiled over my donkey-driving, as I might have smiled over his orthography, or his green tail-coat. But it was not my turn for the moment.

I was proud of my new lore, and thought I had learned the art to perfection. And certainly Modestine did wonders for the rest of the fore-noon, and I had a breathing space to look about me. It was Sabbath; the mountain-fields were all vacant in the sunshine; and as we came down through St. Martin de Frugères, the church was crowded to the door, there were people kneeling without upon the steps, and the sound of the priest's chanting came forth out of the dim interior. It gave me a home feeling on the spot; for I am a countryman of the Sabbath, so to speak, and all Sabbath observances, like a Scottish accent, strike in me mixed feelings, grateful and the reverse. It is only a traveller, hurrying by like a person from another planet, who can rightly enjoy the peace and beauty of the great ascetic feast. The sight of the resting country does his spirit good. There is something better than music in the wide unusual silence; and it disposes him to amiable thoughts, like the sound of a little river or the warmth of sunlight.

In this pleasant humour I came down the hill to where Goudet stands in a green end of a valley, with Chateau Beaufort opposite upon a rocky steep, and the stream, as clear as crystal, lying in a deep pool between them. Above and below, you may hear it wimpling over the stones, an amiable stripling of a river, which it seems absurd to call the Loire. On all sides, Goudet is shut in by mountains; rocky footpaths, practicable at best for donkeys, join it to the outer world of France; and the men and women drink and swear, in their green corner, or look up at the snow-clad peaks in winter from the threshold of their homes, in an isolation, you would think, like that of Homer's Cyclops. But it is not so; the postman reaches Goudet with the letter-bag; the aspiring youth of Goudet are within a day's walk of the railway at Le Puy; and here in the inn you may find an engraved portrait of the host's nephew, Regis Senac, 'Professor of Fencing and Champion of the two Americas,' a distinction gained by him, along with the sum of five hundred dollars, at Tammany Hall, New York, on the 10th April 1876.

I hurried over my midday meal, and was early forth again. But, alas, as we climbed the interminable hill upon the other side, 'Proot!' seemed to have lost its virtue. I prooted like a lion, I prooted mellifluously like a sucking-dove; but Modestine would be neither softened nor intimidated. She held doggedly to her pace; nothing but a blow would move her, and that only

15

for a second. I must follow at her heels, incessantly belabouring. A moment's pause in this ignoble toil, and she relapsed into her own private gait. I think I never heard of any one in as mean a situation. I must reach the lake of Bouchet, where I meant to camp, before sundown, and, to have even a hope of this, I must instantly maltreat this uncomplaining animal. The sound of my own blows sickened me. Once, when I looked at her, she had a faint resemblance to a lady of my acquaintance who formerly loaded me with kindness; and this increased my horror of my cruelty.

To make matters worse, we encountered another donkey, ranging at will upon the roadside; and this other donkey chanced to be a gentleman. He and Modestine met nickering for joy, and I had to separate the pair and beat down their young romance with a renewed and feverish bastinado. If the other donkey had had the heart of a male under his hide, he would have fallen upon me tooth and hoof; and this was a kind of consolation—he was plainly unworthy of Modestine's affection. But the incident saddened me, as did everything that spoke of my donkey's sex.

It was blazing hot up the valley, windless, with vehement sun upon my shoulders; and I had to labour so consistently with my stick that the sweat ran into my eyes. Every five minutes, too, the pack, the basket, and the pilot-coat would take an ugly slew to one side or the other; and I had to stop Modestine, just when I had got her to a tolerable pace of about two miles an hour, to tug, push, shoulder, and readjust the load. And at last, in the village of Ussel, saddle and all, the whole hypothec turned round and grovelled in the dust below the donkey's belly. She, none better pleased, incontinently drew up and seemed to smile; and a party of one man, two women, and two children came up, and, standing round me in a half-circle, encouraged her by their example.

I had the devil's own trouble to get the thing righted; and the instant I had done so, without hesitation, it toppled and fell down upon the other side. Judge if I was hot! And yet not a hand was offered to assist me. The man, indeed, told me I ought to have a package of a different shape. I suggested, if he knew nothing better to the point in my predicament, he might hold his tongue. And the good-natured dog agreed with me smilingly. It was the most despicable fix. I must plainly content myself with the pack for Modestine, and take the following items for my own share of the portage: a cane, a quart-flask, a pilot-jacket heavily weighted in the pockets, two pounds of black bread, and an open basket full of meats and bottles. I believe I may say I am not devoid of greatness of soul; for I did not recoil from this infamous burden. I disposed it, Heaven knows how, so as to be

16

mildly portable, and then proceeded to steer Modestine through the village. She tried, as was indeed her invariable habit, to enter every house and every courtyard in the whole length; and, encumbered as I was, without a hand to help myself, no words can render an idea of my difficulties. A priest, with six or seven others, was examining a church in process of repair, and he and his acolytes laughed loudly as they saw my plight.

I remembered having laughed myself when I had seen good men struggling with adversity in the person of a jackass, and the recollection filled me with penitence. That was in my old light days, before this trouble came upon me. God knows at least that I shall never laugh again, thought I. But oh, what a cruel thing is a farce to those engaged in it! A little out of the village, Modestine, filled with the demon, set her heart upon a by-road, and positively refused to leave it. I dropped all my bundles, and, I am ashamed to say, struck the poor sinner twice across the face. It was pitiful to see her lift her head with shut eyes, as if waiting for another blow. I came very near crying; but I did a wiser thing than that, and sat squarely down by the roadside to consider my situation under the cheerful influence of tobacco and a nip of brandy. Modestine, in the meanwhile, munched some black bread with a contrite hypocritical air. It was plain that I must make a sacrifice to the gods of shipwreck. I threw away the empty bottle destined to carry milk; I threw away my own white bread, and, disdaining to act by general average, kept the black bread for Modestine; lastly, I threw away the cold leg of mutton and the egg-whisk, although this last was dear to my heart. Thus I found room for everything in the basket, and even stowed the boating-coat on the top. By means of an end of cord I slung it under one arm; and although the cord cut my shoulder, and the jacket hung almost to the ground, it was with a heart greatly lightened that I set forth again.

I had now an arm free to thrash Modestine, and cruelly I chastised her. If I were to reach the lakeside before dark, she must bestir her little shanks to some tune. Already the sun had gone down into a windy-looking mist; and although there were still a few streaks of gold far off to the east on the hills and the black fir-woods, all was cold and grey about our onward path. An infinity of little country by-roads led hither and thither among the fields. It was the most pointless labyrinth. I could see my destination overhead, or rather the peak that dominates it; but choose as I pleased, the roads always ended by turning away from it, and sneaking back towards the valley, or northward along the margin of the hills. The failing light, the waning colour, the naked, unhomely, stony country through which I was travelling, threw me into some despondency. I promise you, the stick was not idle; I think every decent step that Modestine took must have cost me at least two emphatic blows. There was not another sound in the neighbourhood but that of my unwearying bastinado.

Suddenly, in the midst of my toils, the load once more bit the dust, and,as by enchantment, all the cords were simultaneously loosened, and the road scattered with my dear possessions. The packing was to begin again from the beginning; and as I had to invent a new and better system, I do not doubt but I lost half an hour. It began to be dusk in earnest as I reached a wilderness of turf and stones. It had the air of being a road which should lead everywhere at the same time; and I was falling into something not unlike despair when I saw two figures stalking towards me over the stones. They walked one behind the other like tramps, but their pace was remarkable. The son led the way, a tall, ill-made, sombre, Scottish-looking man; the mother followed, all in her Sunday's best, with an elegantly embroidered ribbon to her cap, and a new felt hat atop, and proffering, as she strode along with kilted petticoats, a string of obscene and blasphemous oaths.

I hailed the son, and asked him my direction. He pointed loosely west and north-west, muttered an inaudible comment, and, without slackening his pace for an instant, stalked on, as he was going, right athwart my path. The mother followed without so much as raising her head. I shouted and shouted after them, but they continued to scale the hillside, and turned a deaf ear to my outcries. At last, leaving Modestine by herself, I was constrained to run after them, hailing the while. They stopped as I drew near, the mother still cursing; and I could see she was a handsome, motherly, respectable-looking woman. The son once more answered me roughly and inaudibly, and was for setting out again. But this time I simply collared the mother, who was nearest me, and, apologising for my violence, declared that I could not let them go until they had put me on my road. They were neither of them offended—rather mollified than otherwise; told me I had only to follow them; and then the mother asked me what I wanted by the lake at such an hour. I replied, in the Scottish manner, by inquiring if she had far to go herself. She told me, with another oath, that she had an hour and a half's road before her. And then, without salutation, the pair strode forward again up the hillside in the gathering dusk.

I returned for Modestine, pushed her briskly forward, and, after a sharp ascent of twenty minutes, reached the edge of a plateau. The view, looking back on my day's journey, was both wild and sad. Mount Mezenc and the peaks beyond St. Julien stood out in trenchant gloom against a cold glitter

18

in the east; and the intervening field of hills had fallen together into one broad wash of shadow, except here and there the outline of a wooded sugar-loaf in black, here and there a white irregular patch to represent a cultivated farm, and here and there a blot where the Loire, the Gazeille, or the Laussonne wandered in a gorge.

Soon we were on a high-road, and surprise seized on my mind as I beheld a village of some magnitude close at hand; for I had been told that the neighbourhood of the lake was uninhabited except by trout. The road smoked in the twilight with children driving home cattle from the fields; and a pair of mounted stride-legged women, hat and cap and all, dashed past me at a hammering trot from the canton where they had been to church and market. I asked one of the children where I was. At Bouchet St. Nicolas, he told me. Thither, about a mile south of my destination, and on the other side of a respectable summit, had these confused roads and treacherous peasantry conducted me. My shoulder was cut, so that it hurt sharply; my arm ached like toothache from perpetual beating; I gave up the lake and my design to camp, and asked for the auberge.

The Beast of Gevaudan – a contemporary illustration.

Chapter Three

I have a goad

THE AUBERGE OF Bouchet St. Nicolas was among the least pretentious I have ever visited; but I saw many more of the like upon my journey. Indeed, it was typical of these French highlands. Imagine a cottage of two stories, with a bench before the door; the stable and kitchen in a suite, so that Modestine and I could hear each other dining; furniture of the plainest, earthern floors, a single bedchamber for travellers, and that without any convenience but beds. In the kitchen cooking and eating go forward side by side, and the family sleep at night. Any one who has a fancy to wash must do so in public at the common table. The food is sometimes spare; hard fish and omelette have been my portion more than once; the wine is of the smallest, the brandy abominable to man; and the visit of a fat sow, grouting under the table and rubbing against your legs, is no impossible accompaniment to dinner.

But the people of the inn, in nine cases out of ten, show themselves friendly and considerate. As soon as you cross the doors you cease to be a stranger; and although these peasantry are rude and forbidding on the highway, they show a tincture of kind breeding when you share their hearth. At Bouchet, for instance, I uncorked my bottle of Beaujolais, and asked the host to join me. He would take but little. 'I am an amateur of such wine, do you see?' he said, 'and I am capable of leaving you not enough.'

In these hedge-inns the traveller is expected to eat with his own knife; unless he ask, no other will be supplied: with a glass, a whang of bread, and an iron fork, the table is completely laid. My knife was cordially admired by the landlord of Bouchet, and the spring filled him with wonder.

'I should never have guessed that,' he said. 'I would bet,' he added, weighing it in his hand, 'that this cost you not less than five francs.' When I told him it had cost me twenty, his jaw dropped.

He was a mild, handsome, sensible, friendly old man, astonishingly ignorant. His wife, who was not so pleasant in her manners, knew how to read, although I do not suppose she ever did so. She had a share of brains and spoke with a cutting emphasis, like one who ruled the roast.

'My man knows nothing,' she said, with an angry nod; 'he is like the beasts.'

And the old gentleman signified acquiescence with his head. There was no contempt on her part, and no shame on his; the facts were accepted loyally, and no more about the matter.

I was tightly cross-examined about my journey; and the lady understood in a moment, and sketched out what I should put into my book when I got home. 'Whether people harvest or not in such or such a place; if there were forests; studies of manners; what, for example, I and the master of the house say to you; the beauties of Nature, and all that.' And she interrogated me with a look.

'It is just that,' said I.

'You see,' she added to her husband, 'I understood that.'

They were both much interested by the story of my misadventures.

'In the morning,' said the husband, 'I will make you something better than your cane. Such a beast as that feels nothing; it is in the proverb - dur comme un ane; you might beat her insensible with a cudgel, and yet you would arrive nowhere.'

Something better! I little knew what he was offering. The sleeping-room was furnished with two beds. I had one; and I will own I was a little abashed to find a young man and his wife and child in the act of mounting into the other. This was my first experience of the sort; and if I am always to feel equally silly and extraneous, I pray God it be my last as well. I kept my eyes to myself, and know nothing of the woman except that she had beautiful arms, and seemed no whit embarrassed by my appearance. As a matter of fact, the situation was more trying to me than to the pair. A pair keep each other in countenance; it is the single gentleman who has to blush. But I could not help attributing my sentiments to the husband, and sought to conciliate his tolerance with a cup of brandy from my flask. He told me that he was a cooper of Alais travelling to St. Etienne in search of work, and that in his spare moments he followed the fatal calling of a maker of matches. Me, he readily enough divined to be a brandy merchant.

I was up first in the morning (Monday, September 23rd), and hastened my toilette guiltily, so as to leave a clear field for madam, the cooper's wife. I drank a bowl of milk, and set off to explore the neighbourhood of Bouchet. It was perishing cold, a grey, windy, wintry morning; misty clouds flew fast and low; the wind piped over the naked platform; and the only speck of colour was away behind Mount Mezenc and the eastern hills, where the sky still wore the orange of the dawn.

It was five in the morning, and four thousand feet above the sea; and I had to bury my hands in my pockets and trot. People were trooping out to the labours of the field by twos and threes, and all turned round to stare upon the stranger. I had seen them coming back last night, I saw them going afield again; and there was the life of Bouchet in a nutshell.

When I came back to the inn for a bit of breakfast, the landlady was in the kitchen combing out her daughter's hair; and I made her my compliments upon its beauty.

'Oh no,' said the mother; 'it is not so beautiful as it ought to be. Look, it is too fine.'

Thus does a wise peasantry console itself under adverse physica circumstances, and, by a startling democratic process, the defects of the majority decide the type of beauty.

'And where,' said I, 'is monsieur?'

'The master of the house is upstairs,' she answered, 'making you a goad.'

Blessed be the man who invented goads! Blessed the innkeeper of Bouchet St. Nicolas, who introduced me to their use! This plain wand, with an eighth of an inch of pin, was indeed a sceptre when he put it in my hands. Thenceforward Modestine was my slave. A prick, and she passed the most inviting stable door. A prick, and she broke forth into a gallant little trotlet that devoured the miles. It was not a remarkable speed, when all was said; and we took four hours to cover ten miles at the best of it. But what a heavenly change since yesterday! No more wielding of the ugly cudgel; no more flailing with an aching arm; no more broadsword exercise, but a discreet and gentlemanly fence. And what although now and then a drop of blood should appear on Modestine's mouse-coloured wedge-like rump? I should have preferred it otherwise, indeed; but yesterday's exploits had purged my heart of all humanity. The perverse little devil, since she would not be taken with kindness, must even go with pricking.

It was bleak and bitter cold, and, except a cavalcade of stride-legged ladies and a pair of post-runners, the road was dead solitary all the way to Pradelles. I scarce remember an incident but one. A handsome foal with a bell about his neck came charging up to us upon a stretch of common, sniffed the air martially as one about to do great deeds, and suddenly thinking otherwise in his green young heart, put about and galloped off as he had come, the bell tinkling in the wind. For a long while afterwards I saw his noble attitude as he drew up, and heard the note of his bell; and when I struck the high-road, the song of the telegraph-wires seemed to continue the same music.

Pradelles stands on a hillside, high above the Allier, surrounded by rich meadows. They were cutting aftermath on all sides, which gave the neighbourhood, this gusty autumn morning, an untimely smell of hay. On the opposite bank of the Allier the land kept mounting for miles to the horizon: a tanned and sallow autumn landscape, with black blots of fir-wood and white roads wandering through the hills. Over all this the clouds shed a uniform and purplish shadow, sad and somewhat menacing, exaggerating height and distance, and throwing into still higher relief the twisted ribbons of the highway. It was a cheerless prospect, but one stimulating to a traveller. For I was now upon the limit of Velay, and all that I beheld lay in another county - wild Gevaudan, mountainous, uncultivated, and but recently disforested from terror of the wolves.

Wolves, alas, like bandits, seem to flee the traveller's advance; and you may trudge through all our comfortable Europe, and not meet with an adventure worth the name. But here, if anywhere, a man was on the frontiers of hope. For this was the land of the ever-memorable BEAST, the Napoleon Bonaparte of wolves. What a career was his! He lived ten months at free quarters in Gevaudan and Vivarais; he ate women and children and 'shepherdesses celebrated for their beauty'; he pursued armed horsemen; he has been seen at broad noonday chasing a post-chaise and outrider along the king's high-road, and chaise and outrider fleeing before him at the gallop. He was placarded like a political offender, and ten thousand francs were offered for his head. And yet, when he was shot and sent to Versailles, behold! a common wolf, and even small for that. 'Though I could reach from pole to pole,' sang Alexander Pope; the Little Corporal shook Europe; and if all wolves had been as this wolf, they would have changed the history of man. M. Elie Berthet has made him the hero of a novel, which I have read, and do not wish to read again.

I hurried over my lunch, and was proof against the landlady's desire that I should visit our Lady of Pradelles, 'who performed many miracles, although she was of wood'; and before three-quarters of an hour I was goading Modestine down the steep descent that leads to Langogne on the Allier. On both sides of the road, in big dusty fields, farmers were preparing for next spring. Every fifty yards a yoke of great-necked stolid oxen were patiently haling at the plough. I saw one of these mild formidable servants of the glebe, who took a sudden interest in Modestine and me. The furrow down which he was journeying lay at an angle to the road, and his head was solidly fixed to the yoke like those of caryatides below a ponderous cornice; but he screwed round his big honest eyes and followed us with a ruminating look, until his master bade him turn the plough and proceed to reascend the field. From all these furrowing ploughshares, from the feet of oxen, from a labourer here and there who was breaking the dry clods with a hoe, the wind carried away a thin dust like so much smoke. It was a fine, busy, breathing, rustic landscape; and as I continued to descend, the highlands of Gevaudan kept mounting in front of me against the sky.

I had crossed the Loire the day before; now I was to cross the Allier; so near are these two confluents in their youth. Just at the bridge of Langogne, as the long-promised rain was beginning to fall, a lassie of some seven or eight addressed me in the sacramental phrase, 'D'ou'st-ce-que vous venez?' She did it with so high an air that she set me laughing; and this cut her to the quick. She was evidently one who reckoned on respect, and stood looking after me in silent dudgeon, as I crossed the bridge and entered the county of Gevaudan.

Upper Gevaudan

The way also here was very wearisome through dirt and slabbiness; nor was there on all this ground so much as one inn or victualling-house wherein to refresh the feebler sort.

PILGRIM'S PROGRESS

Chapter Four

A camp
in the dark

T HE NEXT DAY (Tuesday, September 24th), it was two o'clock in the afternoon before I got my journal written up and my knapsack repaired, for I was determined to carry my knapsack in the future and have no more ado with baskets; and half an hour afterwards I set out for Le Cheylard l'Eveque, a place on the borders of the forest of Mercoire. A man, I was told, should walk there in an hour and a half; and I thought it scarce too ambitious to suppose that a man encumbered with a donkey might cover the same distance in four hours.

All the way up the long hill from Langogne it rained and hailed alternately; the wind kept freshening steadily, although slowly; plentiful hurrying clouds - some dragging veils of straight rain-shower, others massed and luminous as though promising snow - careered out of the north and followed me along my way. I was soon out of the cultivated basin of the Allier, and away from the ploughing oxen, and such-like sights of the country. Moor, heathery marsh, tracts of rock and pines, woods of birch all jewelled with the autumn yellow, here and there a few naked cottages and bleak fields, - these were the characters of the country. Hill and valley followed valley and hill; the little green and stony cattle-tracks wandered in and out of one another, split into three or four, died away in marshy hollows, and began again sporadically on hillsides or at the borders of a wood. There was no direct road to Cheylard, and it was no easy affair to make a passage in this uneven country and through this intermittent labyrinth of tracks. It must have been about four when I struck Sagnerousse, and went on my way rejoicing in a sure point of departure. Two hours afterwards, the dusk rapidly falling, in a lull of the wind, I issued from a fir-wood where I had long been wandering, and found, not the looked-for village, but another marish bottom among rough-and-tumble hills. For some time past I had heard the ringing of cattle-bells ahead; and now, as I came out of the skirts of the wood, I saw near upon a dozen cows and perhaps as many more black figures, which I conjectured to be children, although the mist had almost unrecognisably exaggerated their forms. These were all silently following each other round and round in a circle, now taking hands, now breaking up with chains and reverences. A dance of children appeals to very innocent and lively thoughts; but, at nightfall on the marshes, the thing was eerie and fantastic to behold. Even I, who am well enough read in Herbert Spencer, felt a sort of silence fall for an instant on my mind. The next, I was pricking Modestine forward, and guiding her like an unruly ship through the open. In a path, she went doggedly ahead of her own accord, as before a fair wind; but once on the turf or among heather, and the brute became demented. The tendency of lost travellers to go round in a circle was developed in her to the degree of passion, and it took all the steering I had in me to keep even a decently straight course through a single field.

While I was thus desperately tacking through the bog, children and cattle began to disperse, until only a pair of girls remained behind. From these I sought direction on my path. The peasantry in general were but little disposed to counsel a wayfarer. One old devil simply retired into his house, and barricaded the door on my approach; and I might beat and shout myself hoarse, he turned a deaf ear. Another, having given me a direction which, as I found afterwards, I had misunderstood, complacently watched me going wrong without adding a sign. He did not care a stalk of parsley if I wandered all night upon the hills! As for these two girls, they were a pair of impudent sly sluts, with not a thought but mischief. One put out her tongue at me, the other bade me follow the cows; and they both giggled and jogged each other's elbows. The Beast of Gevaudan ate about a hundred children of this district; I began to think of him with sympathy.

Leaving the girls, I pushed on through the bog, and got into another wood and upon a well-marked road. It grew darker and darker. Modestine, suddenly beginning to smell mischief, bettered the pace of her own accord, and from that time forward gave me no trouble. It was the first sign of intelligence I had occasion to remark in her. At the same time, the wind freshened into half a gale, and another heavy discharge of rain came flying up out of the north. At the other side of the wood I sighted some red windows in the dusk. This was the hamlet of Fouzilhic; three houses on a hillside, near a wood of birches. Here I found a delightful old man, who came a little way with me in the rain to put me safely on the road for Cheylard. He would hear of no reward; but shook his hands above his head almost as if in menace, and refused volubly and shrilly, in unmitigated patois.

All seemed right at last. My thoughts began to turn upon dinner and a fireside, and my heart was agreeably softened in my bosom. Alas, and I was on the brink of new and greater miseries! Suddenly, at a single swoop, the night fell. I have been abroad in many a black night, but never in a blacker. A glimmer of rocks, a glimmer of the track where it was well beaten, a certain fleecy density, or night within night, for a tree, - this was all that I could discriminate. The sky was simply darkness overhead; even the flying clouds pursued their way invisibly to human eyesight. I could not distinguish my hand at arm's-length from the track, nor my goad, at the same distance, from the meadows or the sky.

Soon the road that I was following split, after the fashion of the country, into three or four in a piece of rocky meadow. Since Modestine had shown such a fancy for beaten roads, I tried her instinct in this predicament. But the instinct of an ass is what might be expected from the name; in half a minute she was clambering round and round among some boulders, as lost a donkey as you would wish to see. I should have camped long before had I been properly provided; but as this was to be so short a stage, I had brought no wine, no bread for myself, and little over a pound for my lady friend. Add to this, that I and Modestine were both handsomely wetted by the showers. But now, if I could have found some water, I should have camped at once in spite of all. Water, however, being entirely absent, except in the form of rain, I determined to return to Fouzilhic, and ask a guide a little farther on my way - 'a little farther lend thy guiding hand.'

The thing was easy to decide, hard to accomplish. In this sensible roaring blackness I was sure of nothing but the direction of the wind. To this I set my face; the road had disappeared, and I went across country, now in marshy opens, now baffled by walls unscalable to Modestine, until I came once more in sight of some red windows. This time they were differently disposed. It was not Fouzilhic, but Fouzilhac, a hamlet little distant from the other in space, but worlds away in the spirit of its inhabitants. I tied Modestine to a gate, and groped forward, stumbling among rocks, plunging mid-leg in bog, until I gained the entrance of the village. In the first lighted house there was a woman who would not open to me. She could do nothing, she cried to me through the door, being alone and lame; but if I would apply at the next house, there was a man who could help me if he had a mind.

They came to the next door in force, a man, two women, and a girl, and brought a pair of lanterns to examine the wayfarer. The man was not ill-looking, but had a shifty smile. He leaned against the doorpost, and heard me state my case. All I asked was a guide as far as Cheylard.

'C'est que, voyez-vous, il fait noir,' said he.

I told him that was just my reason for requiring help.

'I understand that,' said he, looking uncomfortable; 'mais - c'est de la peine.'

I was willing to pay, I said.

He shook his head. I rose as high as ten francs; but he continued to shake his head.

'Name your own price, then,' said I.

'Ce n'est pas ca,' he said at length, and with evident difficulty; 'but I am not going to cross the door - mais je ne sortirai pas de la porte.'

I grew a little warm, and asked him what he proposed that I should do.

'Where are you going beyond Cheylard?' he asked by way of answer.

'That is no affair of yours,' I returned, for I was not going to indulge his bestial curiosity; 'it changes nothing in my present predicament.'

'C'est vrai, ca,' he acknowledged, with a laugh; 'oui, c'est vrai. Et d'ou venez-vous?'

A better man than I might have felt nettled.

'Oh,' said I, 'I am not going to answer any of your questions, so you may spare yourself the trouble of putting them. I am late enough already; I want help. If you will not guide me yourself, at least help me to find some one else who will.'

'Hold on,' he cried suddenly. 'Was it not you who passed in the meadow while it was still day?'

'Yes, yes,' said the girl, whom I had not hitherto recognised; 'it was monsieur; I told him to follow the cow.'

'As for you, mademoiselle,' said I, 'you are a farceuse.'

'And,' added the man, 'what the devil have you done to be still here?'

What the devil, indeed! But there I was.

'The great thing,' said I, 'is to make an end of it'; and once more proposed that he should help me to find a guide.

'C'est que,' he said again, 'c'est que - il fait noir.'

'Very well,' said I; 'take one of your lanterns.'

'No,' he cried, drawing a thought backward, and again intrenching himself behind one of his former phrases; 'I will not cross the door.'

I looked at him. I saw unaffected terror struggling on his face with unaffected shame; he was smiling pitifully and wetting his lip with his tongue, like a detected schoolboy. I drew a brief picture of my state, and asked him what I was to do.

'I don't know,' he said; 'I will not cross the door.'

Here was the Beast of Gevaudan, and no mistake.

'Sir,' said I, with my most commanding manners, 'you are a coward.'

And with that I turned my back upon the family party, who hastened to retire within their fortifications; and the famous door was closed again, but not till I had overheard the sound of laughter.

Filia barbara pater barbarior. Let me say it in the plural: the Beasts of Gevaudan.

The lanterns had somewhat dazzled me, and I ploughed distressfully among stones and rubbish-heaps. All the other houses in the village were both dark and silent; and though I knocked at here and there a door, my knocking was unanswered. It was a bad business; I gave up Fouzilhac with my curses. The rain had stopped, and the wind, which still kept rising, began to dry my coat and trousers. 'Very well,' thought I, 'water or no water, I must camp.' But the first thing was to return to Modestine. I am pretty sure I was twenty minutes groping for my lady in the dark; and if it had not been for the unkindly services of the bog, into which I once more stumbled, I might have still been groping for her at the dawn. My next business was to gain the shelter of a wood, for the wind was cold as well as boisterous. How, in this well-wooded district, I should have been so long in finding one, is another of the insoluble mysteries of this day's adventures; but I will take my oath that I put near an hour to the discovery.

At last black trees began to show upon my left, and, suddenly crossing the road, made a cave of unmitigated blackness right in front. I call it a cave without exaggeration; to pass below that arch of leaves was like entering a dungeon. I felt about until my hand encountered a stout branch, and to this I tied Modestine, a haggard, drenched, desponding donkey. Then I lowered my pack, laid it along the wall on the margin of the road, and unbuckled the straps. I knew well enough where the lantern was; but where were the candles? I groped and groped among the tumbled articles, and, while I was thus groping, suddenly I touched the spirit-lamp. Salvation! This would serve my turn as well. The wind roared unwearyingly among the trees; I could hear the boughs tossing and the leaves churning through half a mile of forest; yet the scene of my encampment was not only as black as the pit, but admirably sheltered. At the second match the wick caught flame. The light was both livid and shifting; but it cut me off from the universe, and doubled the darkness of the surrounding night.

I tied Modestine more conveniently for herself, and broke up half the black bread for her supper, reserving the other half against the morning. Then I gathered what I should want within reach, took off my wet boots and gaiters, which I wrapped in my waterproof, arranged my knapsack for a pillow under the flap of my sleeping-bag, insinuated my limbs into the interior, and buckled myself in like a bambino. I opened a tin of Bologna sausage and broke a cake of chocolate, and that was all I had to eat. It may sound offensive, but I ate them together, bite by bite, by way of bread and meat. All I had to wash down this revolting mixture was neat brandy: a revolting beverage in itself. But I was rare and hungry; ate well, and

32

smoked one of the best cigarettes in my experience. Then I put a stone in my straw hat, pulled the flap of my fur cap over my neck and eyes, put my revolver ready to my hand, and snuggled well down among the sheepskins.

I questioned at first if I were sleepy, for I felt my heart beating faster than usual, as if with an agreeable excitement to which my mind remained a stranger. But as soon as my eyelids touched, that subtle glue leaped between them, and they would no more come separate. The wind among the trees was my lullaby. Sometimes it sounded for minutes together with a steady, even rush, not rising nor abating; and again it would swell and burst like a great crashing breaker, and the trees would patter me all over with big drops from the rain of the afternoon. Night after night, in my own bedroom in the country, I have given ear to this perturbing concert of the wind among the woods; but whether it was a difference in the trees, or the lie of the ground, or because I was myself outside and in the midst of it, the fact remains that the wind sang to a different tune among these woods of Gevaudan. I hearkened and hearkened; and meanwhile sleep took gradual possession of my body and subdued my thoughts and senses; but still my last waking effort was to listen and distinguish, and my last conscious state was one of wonder at the foreign clamour in my ears.

Twice in the course of the dark hours - once when a stone galled me underneath the sack, and again when the poor patient Modestine, growing angry, pawed and stamped upon the road - I was recalled for a brief while to consciousness, and saw a star or two overhead, and the lace-like edge of the foliage against the sky. When I awoke for the third time (Wednesday, September 25th), the world was flooded with a blue light, the mother of the dawn. I saw the leaves labouring in the wind and the ribbon of the road; and, on turning my head, there was Modestine tied to a beech, and standing half across the path in an attitude of inimitable patience. I closed my eyes again, and set to thinking over the experience of the night. I was surprised to find how easy and pleasant it had been, even in this tempestuous weather. The stone which annoyed me would not have been there, had I not been forced to camp blindfold in the opaque night; and I had felt no other inconvenience, except when my feet encountered the lantern or the second volume of Peyrat's Pastors of the Desert among the mixed contents of my sleeping-bag; nay, more, I had felt not a touch of cold, and awakened with unusually lightsome and clear sensations.

With that, I shook myself, got once more into my boots and gaiters, and, breaking up the rest of the bread for Modestine, strolled about to see in what part of the world I had awakened. Ulysses, left on Ithaca, and with a mind unsettled by the goddess, was not more pleasantly astray. I have been after an adventure all my life, a pure dispassionate adventure, such as befell early and heroic voyagers; and thus to be found by morning in a random woodside nook in Gevaudan - not knowing north from south, as strange to my surroundings as the first man upon the earth, an inland castaway - was to find a fraction of my day-dreams realised. I was on the skirts of a little wood of birch, sprinkled with a few beeches; behind, it adjoined another wood of fir; and in front, it broke up and went down in open order into a shallow and meadowy dale. All around there were bare hilltops, some near, some far away, as the perspective closed or opened, but none apparently much higher than the rest. The wind huddled the trees. The golden specks of autumn in the birches tossed shiveringly. Overhead the sky was full of strings and shreds of vapour, flying, vanishing, reappearing, and turning about an axis like tumblers, as the wind hounded them through heaven. It was wild weather and famishing cold. I ate some chocolate, swallowed a mouthful of brandy, and smoked a cigarette before the cold should have time to disable my fingers. And by the time I had got all this done, and had made my pack and bound it on the pack-saddle, the day was tiptoe on the threshold of the east. We had not gone many steps along the lane, before the sun, still invisible to me, sent a glow of gold over some cloud mountains that lay ranged along the eastern sky.

The wind had us on the stern, and hurried us bitingly forward. I buttoned myself into my coat, and walked on in a pleasant frame of mind with all men, when suddenly, at a corner, there was Fouzilhic once more in front of me. Nor only that, but there was the old gentleman who had escorted me so far the night before, running out of his house at sight of me, with hands upraised in horror.

'My poor boy!' he cried, 'what does this mean?'

I told him what had happened. He beat his old hands like clappers in a mill, to think how lightly he had let me go; but when he heard of the man of Fouzilhac, anger and depression seized upon his mind.

'This time, at least,' said he, 'there shall be no mistake.'

And he limped along, for he was very rheumatic, for about half a mile, and until I was almost within sight of Cheylard, the destination I had hunted for so long.

Chapter Five

Cheylard
and Luc

CANDIDLY, IT SEEMED little worthy of all this searching. A few broken ends of village, with no particular street, but a succession of open places heaped with logs and fagots; a couple of tilted crosses, a shrine to Our Lady of all Graces on the summit of a little hill; and all this, upon a rattling highland river, in the corner of a naked valley. What went ye out for to see? thought I to myself. But the place had a life of its own. I found a board, commemorating the liberalities of Cheylard for the past year, hung up, like a banner, in the diminutive and tottering church. In 1877, it appeared, the inhabitants subscribed forty-eight francs ten centimes for the 'Work of the Propagation of the Faith.' Some of this, I could not help hoping, would be applied to my native land. Cheylard scrapes together halfpence for the darkened souls in Edinburgh; while Balquhidder and Dunrossness bemoan the ignorance of Rome. Thus, to the high entertainment of the angels, do we pelt each other with evangelists, like schoolboys bickering in the snow.

The inn was again singularly unpretentious. The whole furniture of a not ill-to-do family was in the kitchen: the beds, the cradle, the clothes, the plate-rack, the meal-chest, and the photograph of the parish priest. There were five children, one of whom was set to its morning prayers at the stair-foot soon after my arrival, and a sixth would ere long be forthcoming. I was kindly received by these good folk. They were much interested in my misadventure. The wood in which I had slept belonged to them; the man of Fouzilhac they thought a monster of iniquity, and counselled me warmly to summon him at law - 'because I might have died.' The good wife was horror-stricken to see me drink over a pint of uncreamed milk.

'You will do yourself an evil,' she said. 'Permit me to boil it for you.'

After I had begun the morning on this delightful liquor, she having an infinity of things to arrange, I was permitted, nay requested, to make a bowl of chocolate for myself. My boots and gaiters were hung up to dry, and, seeing me trying to write my journal on my knee, the eldest daughter let down a hinged table in the chimney-corner for my convenience. Here I wrote, drank my chocolate, and finally ate an omelette before I left. The table was thick with dust; for, as they explained, it was not used except in winter weather. I had a clear look up the vent, through brown agglomerations of soot and blue vapour, to the sky; and whenever a handful of twigs was thrown on to the fire, my legs were scorched by the blaze.

The husband had begun life as a muleteer, and when I came to charge Modestine showed himself full of the prudence of his art. 'You will have to change this package,' said he; 'it ought to be in two parts, and then you might have double the weight.'

I explained that I wanted no more weight; and for no donkey hitherto created would I cut my sleeping-bag in two.

'It fatigues her, however,' said the innkeeper; 'it fatigues her greatly on the march. Look.'

Alas, there were her two forelegs no better than raw beef on the inside and blood was running from under her tail. They told me when I started, and I was ready to believe it, that before a few days I should come to love Modestine like a dog. Three days had passed, we had shared some misadventures, and my heart was still as cold as a potato towards my beast of burden. She was pretty enough to look at; but then she had given proof of dead stupidity, redeemed indeed by patience, but aggravated by flashes of sorry and ill-judged light-heartedness. And I own this new discovery seemed another point against her. What the devil was the good of a she-ass

The "diminutive and tottering church" at Chelylard.

if she could not carry a sleeping-bag and a few necessaries? I saw the end of the fable rapidly approaching, when I should have to carry Modestine.

Aesop was the man to know the world! I assure you I set out with heavy thoughts upon my short day's march.

It was not only heavy thoughts about Modestine that weighted me upon the way; it was a leaden business altogether. For first, the wind blew so rudely that I had to hold on the pack with one hand from Cheylard to Luc; and second, my road lay through one of the most beggarly countries in the world. It was like the worst of the Scottish Highlands, only worse; cold, naked, and ignoble, scant of wood, scant of heather, scant of life. A road and some fences broke the unvarying waste, and the line of the road was marked by upright pillars, to serve in time of snow.

Why any one should desire to visit either Luc or Cheylard is more than my much-inventing spirit can suppose. For my part, I travel not to go anywhere, but to go. I travel for travel's sake. The great affair is to move; to feel the needs and hitches of our life more nearly; to come down off this feather-bed of civilisation, and find the globe granite underfoot and strewn with cutting flints. Alas, as we get up in life, and are more preoccupied with our affairs, even a holiday is a thing that must be worked for. To hold a pack upon a pack-saddle against a gale out of the freezing north is no high industry, but it is one that serves to occupy and compose the mind. And when the present is so exacting, who can annoy himself about the future?

I came out at length above the Allier. A more unsightly prospect at this season of the year it would be hard to fancy. Shelving hills rose round it on all sides, here dabbled with wood and fields, there rising to peaks alternately naked and hairy with pines. The colour throughout was black or ashen, and came to a point in the ruins of the castle of Luc, which pricked up impudently from below my feet, carrying on a pinnacle a tall white statue of Our Lady, which, I heard with interest, weighed fifty quintals, and was to be dedicated on the 6th of October. Through this sorry landscape trickled the Allier and a tributary of nearly equal size, which came down to join it through a broad nude valley in Vivarais. The weather had somewhat lightened, and the clouds massed in squadron; but the fierce wind still hunted them through heaven, and cast great ungainly splashes of shadow and sunlight over the scene.

Luc itself was a straggling double file of houses wedged between hill and river. It had no beauty, nor was there any notable feature, save the old castle overhead with its fifty quintals of brand-new Madonna. But the inn was clean and large.

The kitchen, with its two box-beds hung with clean check curtains, with its wide stone chimney, its chimney-shelf four yards long and garnished with lanterns and religious statuettes, its array of chests and pair of ticking clocks, was the very model of what a kitchen ought to be; a melodrama kitchen, suitable for bandits or noblemen in disguise. Nor was the scene disgraced by the landlady, a handsome, silent, dark old woman, clothed and hooded in black like a nun. Even the public bedroom had a character of its own, with the long deal tables and benches, where fifty might have dined, set out as for a harvest-home, and the three box-beds along the wall. In one of these, lying on straw and covered with a pair of table-napkins, did I do penance all night long in goose-flesh and chattering teeth, and sigh, from time to time as I awakened, for my sheepskin sack and the lee of some great wood.

Our Lady of the Snows

'I behold the House,
    The Brotherhood austere –
And what am I,
    That I am here?'

MATTHEW ARNOLD

Chapter Six

Father Apollinaris

NEXT MORNING (Thursday, 26th September) I took the road in a new order. The sack was no longer doubled, but hung at full length across the saddle, a green sausage six feet long with a tuft of blue wool hanging out of either end. It was more picturesque, it spared the donkey, and, as I began to see, it would ensure stability, blow high, blow low. But it was not without a pang that I had so decided. For although I had purchased a new cord, and made all as fast as I was able, I was yet jealously uneasy lest the flaps should tumble out and scatter my effects along the line of march.

My way lay up the bald valley of the river, along the march of Vivarais and Gevaudan. The hills of Gevaudan on the right were a little more naked, if anything, than those of Vivarais upon the left, and the former had a monopoly of a low dotty underwood that grew thickly in the gorges and died out in solitary burrs upon the shoulders and the summits. Black bricks of fir-wood were plastered here and there upon both sides, and here and there were cultivated fields. A railway ran beside the river; the only bit of railway in Gevaudan, although there are many proposals afoot and surveys being made, and even, as they tell me, a station standing ready built in Mende. A year or two hence and this may be another world. The desert is beleaguered. Now may some

Languedocian Wordsworth turn the sonnet into patois: 'Mountains and vales and floods, heard YE that whistle?'

At a place called La Bastide I was directed to leave the river, and follow a road that mounted on the left among the hills of Vivarais, the modern Ardeche; for I was now come within a little way of my strange destination, the Trappist monastery of Our Lady of the Snows. The sun came out as I left the shelter of a pine-wood, and I beheld suddenly a fine wild landscape to the south. High rocky hills, as blue as sapphire, closed the view, and between these lay ridge upon ridge, heathery, craggy, the sun glittering on veins of rock, the underwood clambering in the hollows, as rude as God made them at the first. There was not a sign of man's hand in all the prospect; and indeed not a trace of his passage, save where generation after generation had walked in twisted footpaths, in and out among the beeches, and up and down upon the channelled slopes. The mists, which had hitherto beset me, were now broken into clouds, and fled swiftly and shone brightly in the sun. I drew a long breath. It was grateful to come, after so long, upon a scene of some attraction for the human heart. I own I like definite form in what my eyes are to rest upon; and if landscapes were sold, like the sheets of characters of my boyhood, one penny plain and twopence coloured, I should go the length of twopence every day of my life.

But if things had grown better to the south, it was still desolate and inclement near at hand. A spidery cross on every hill-top marked the neighbourhood of a religious house; and a quarter of a mile beyond, the outlook southward opening out and growing bolder with every step, a white statue of the Virgin at the corner of a young plantation directed the traveller to Our Lady of the Snows. Here, then, I struck leftward, and pursued my way, driving my secular donkey before me, and creaking in my secular boots and gaiters, towards the asylum of silence.

I had not gone very far ere the wind brought to me the clanging of a bell, and somehow, I can scarce tell why, my heart sank within me at the sound. I have rarely approached anything with more unaffected terror than the monastery of Our Lady of the Snows. This it is to have had a Protestant education. And suddenly, on turning a corner, fear took hold on me from head to foot - slavish, superstitious fear; and though I did not stop in my advance, yet I went on slowly, like a man who should have passed a bourne unnoticed, and strayed into the country of the dead. For there, upon the narrow new-made road, between the stripling pines, was a mediaeval friar, fighting with a barrowful of turfs. Every Sunday of my childhood I used to study the Hermits of Marco Sadeler—enchanting prints, full of wood and field and mediaeval landscapes, as large as a county, for the imagination to go a-travelling in; and here, sure enough, was one of Marco Sadeler's heroes. He was robed in white like any spectre, and the hood falling back, in the instancy of his contention with the barrow, disclosed a pate as bald and yellow as a skull. He might have been buried any time these thousand years, and all the lively parts of him resolved into earth and broken up with the farmer's harrow.

I was troubled besides in my mind as to etiquette. Durst I address a person who was under a vow of silence? Clearly not. But drawing near, I doffed my cap to him with a far-away superstitious reverence. He nodded back, and cheerfully addressed me. Was I going to the monastery? Who was I? An Englishman? Ah, an Irishman, then?

'No,' I said, 'a Scotsman.'

A Scotsman? Ah, he had never seen a Scotsman before. And he looked me all over, his good, honest, brawny countenance shining with interest, as a boy might look upon a lion or an alligator. From him I learned with disgust that I could not be received at Our Lady of the Snows; I might get a meal, perhaps, but that was all. And then, as our talk ran on, and it turned out that I was not a pedlar, but a literary man, who drew landscapes and was going to write a book, he changed his manner of thinking as to my reception (for I fear they respect persons even in a Trappist monastery), and told me I must be sure to ask for the Father Prior, and state my case to him in full. On second thoughts he determined to go down with me himself; he thought he could manage for me better. Might he say that I was a geographer?

No; I thought, in the interests of truth, he positively might not.

'Very well, then' (with disappointment), 'an author.'

It appeared he had been in a seminary with six young Irishmen, all priests long since, who had received newspapers and kept him informed of the state of ecclesiastical affairs in England. And he asked me eagerly after Dr. Pusey, for whose conversion the good man had continued ever since to pray night and morning.

'I thought he was very near the truth,' he said; 'and he will reach it yet; there is so much virtue in prayer.'

He must be a stiff, ungodly Protestant who can take anything but pleasure in this kind and hopeful story. While he was thus near the subject, the good father asked me if I were a Christian; and when he found I was not, or not after his way, he glossed it over with great good-will. The road which we were following, and which this stalwart father had made with his own two hands within the space of a year, came to a corner, and showed us some white buildings a little farther on beyond the wood. At the same time, the bell once more sounded abroad. We were hard upon the monastery. Father Apollinaris (for that was my companion's name) stopped me.

'I must not speak to you down there,' he said. 'Ask for the Brother Porter, and all will be well. But try to see me as you go out again through the wood, where I may speak to you. I am charmed to have made your acquaintance.'

And then suddenly raising his arms, flapping his fingers, and crying out twice, 'I must not speak, I must not speak!' he ran away in front of me, and disappeared into the monastery door.

I own this somewhat ghastly eccentricity went a good way to revive my terrors. But where one was so good and simple, why should not all be alike? I took heart of grace, and went forward to the gate as fast as Modestine, who seemed to have a disaffection for monasteries, would permit. It was the first door, in my acquaintance of her, which she had not shown an indecent haste to enter. I summoned the place in form, though with a quaking heart. Father Michael, the Father Hospitaller, and a pair of brown-robed brothers came to the gate and spoke with me a while. I think my sack was the great attraction; it had already beguiled the heart of poor Apollinaris, who had charged me on my life to show it to the Father Prior. But whether it was my address, or the sack, or the idea speedily published among that part of the brotherhood who attend on strangers that I was not a pedlar after all, I found no difficulty as to my reception. Modestine was led away by a layman to the stables, and I and my pack were received into Our Lady of the Snows.

Chapter Seven

The monks

FATHER MICHAEL, a pleasant, fresh-faced, smiling man, perhaps of thirty-five, took me to the pantry, and gave me a glass of liqueur to stay me until dinner. We had some talk, or rather I should say he listened to my prattle indulgently enough, but with an abstracted air, like a spirit with a thing of clay. And truly, when I remember that I descanted principally on my appetite, and that it must have been by that time more than eighteen hours since Father Michael had so much as broken bread, I can well understand that he would find an earthly savour in my conversation. But his manner, though superior, was exquisitely gracious; and I find I have a lurking curiosity as to Father Michael's past.

The whet administered, I was left alone for a little in the monastery garden. This is no more than the main court, laid out in sandy paths and beds of parti-coloured dahlias, and with a fountain and a black statue of the Virgin in the centre. The buildings stand around it four-square, bleak, as yet unseasoned by the years and weather, and with no other features than a belfry and a pair of slated gables. Brothers in white, brothers in brown, passed silently along the sanded alleys; and when I first came out, three hooded monks were kneeling on the terrace at their prayers. A naked hill commands the monastery upon one side, and the wood commands it on the other. It lies exposed to wind; the snow falls off and on from October to May, and sometimes lies six weeks on end; but if they stood in

Eden, with a climate like heaven's, the buildings themselves would offer the same wintry and cheerless aspect; and for my part, on this wild September day, before I was called to dinner, I felt chilly in and out.

When I had eaten well and heartily, Brother Ambrose, a hearty conversible Frenchman (for all those who wait on strangers have the liberty to speak), led me to a little room in that part of the building which is set apart for MM. les retraitants. It was clean and whitewashed, and furnished with strict necessaries, a crucifix, a bust of the late Pope, the Imitation in French, a book of religious meditations, and the Life of Elizabeth Seton, evangelist, it would appear, of North America and of New England in particular. As far as my experience goes, there is a fair field for some more evangelisation in these quarters; but think of Cotton Mather! I should like to give him a reading of this little work in heaven, where I hope he dwells; but perhaps he knows all that already, and much more; and perhaps he and Mrs. Seton are the dearest friends, and gladly unite their voices in the everlasting psalm. Over the table, to conclude the inventory of the room, hung a set of regulations for MM. les retraitants: what services they should attend, when they were to tell their beads or meditate, and when they were to rise and go to rest. At the foot was a notable N.B.: 'Le temps libre est employe a l'examen de conscience, a la confession, a faire de bonnes resolutions, etc.' To make good resolutions, indeed! You might talk as fruitfully of making the hair grow on your head.

I had scarce explored my niche when Brother Ambrose returned. An English boarder, it appeared, would like to speak with me. I professed my willingness, and the friar ushered in a fresh, young, little Irishman of fifty, a deacon of the Church, arrayed in strict canonicals, and wearing on his head what, in default of knowledge, I can only call the ecclesiastical shako. He had lived seven years in retreat at a convent of nuns in Belgium, and now five at Our Lady of the Snows; he never saw an English newspaper; he spoke French imperfectly, and had he spoken it like a native, there was not much chance of conversation where he dwelt. With this, he was a man eminently sociable, greedy of news, and simple-minded like a child. If I was pleased to have a guide about the monastery, he was no less delighted to see an English face and hear an English tongue.

He showed me his own room, where he passed his time among breviaries, Hebrew Bibles, and the Waverley Novels. Thence he led me to the cloisters, into the chapter-house, through the vestry, where the brothers' gowns and broad straw hats were hanging up, each with his religious name upon a board - names full of legendary suavity and interest, such as Basil,

Hilarion, Raphael, or Pacifique; into the library, where were all the works of Veuillot and Chateaubriand, and the Odes et Ballades, if you please, and even Moliere, to say nothing of innumerable fathers and a great variety of local and general historians. Thence my good Irishman took me round the workshops, where brothers bake bread, and make cartwheels, and take photographs; where one superintends a collection of curiosities, and another a gallery of rabbits. For in a Trappist monastery each monk has an occupation of his own choice, apart from his religious duties and the general labours of the house. Each must sing in the choir, if he has a voice and ear, and join in the haymaking if he has a hand to stir; but in his private hours, although he must be occupied, he may be occupied on what he likes. Thus I was told that one brother was engaged with literature; while Father Apollinaris busies himself in making roads, and the Abbot employs himself in binding books. It is not so long since this Abbot was consecrated, by the way; and on that occasion, by a special grace, his mother was permitted to enter the chapel and witness the ceremony of consecration. A proud day for her to have a son a mitred abbot; it makes you glad to think they let her in.

In all these journeyings to and fro, many silent fathers and brethren fell in our way. Usually they paid no more regard to our passage than if we had been a cloud; but sometimes the good deacon had a permission to ask of them, and it was granted by a peculiar movement of the hands, almost like that of a dog's paws in swimming, or refused by the usual negative signs, and in either case with lowered eyelids and a certain air of contrition, as of a man who was steering very close to evil.

The monks, by special grace of their Abbot, were still taking two meals a day; but it was already time for their grand fast, which begins somewhere in September and lasts till Easter, and during which they eat but once in the twenty-four hours, and that at two in the afternoon, twelve hours after they have begun the toil and vigil of the day. Their meals are scanty, but even of these they eat sparingly; and though each is allowed a small carafe of wine, many refrain from this indulgence. Without doubt, the most of mankind grossly overeat themselves; our meals serve not only for support, but as a hearty and natural diversion from the labour of life. Yet, though excess may be hurtful, I should have thought this Trappist regimen defective. And I am astonished, as I look back, at the freshness of face and cheerfulness of manner of all whom I beheld. A happier nor a healthier company I should scarce suppose that I have ever seen. As a matter of fact, on this bleak upland, and with the incessant occupation of the monks, life is of an uncertain tenure, and death no infrequent visitor, at Our Lady of the Snows. This, at least, was what was told me. But if they die easily, they must live healthily in the meantime, for they seemed all firm of flesh and high in colour; and the only morbid sign that I could observe, an unusual brilliancy of eye, was one that served rather to increase the general impression of vivacity and strength.

Those with whom I spoke were singularly sweet-tempered, with what I can only call a holy cheerfulness in air and conversation. There is a note, in the direction to visitors, telling them not to be offended at the curt speech of those who wait upon them, since it is proper to monks to speak little. The note might have been spared; to a man the hospitallers were all brimming with innocent talk and, in my experience of the monastery, it was easier to begin than to break off a conversation. With the exception of Father Michael, who was a man of the world, they showed themselves full of kind and healthy interest in all sorts of subjects—in politics, in voyages, in my sleeping-sack - and not without a certain pleasure in the sound of their own voices.

As for those who are restricted to silence, I can only wonder how they bear their solemn and cheerless isolation. And yet, apart from any view of mortification, I can see a certain policy, not only in the exclusion of women, but in this vow of silence. I have had some experience of lay phalansteries, of an artistic, not to say a bacchanalian character; and seen more than one association easily formed and yet more easily dispersed. With a Cistercian rule, perhaps they might have lasted longer. In the neighbourhood of women it is but a touch-and-go association that can be formed among defenceless men; the stronger electricity is sure to triumph; the dreams of boyhood, the schemes of youth, are abandoned after an interview of ten minutes, and the arts and sciences, and professional male jollity, deserted at once for two sweet eyes and a caressing accent. And next after this, the tongue is the
great divider.

I am almost ashamed to pursue this worldly criticism of a religious rule; but there is yet another point in which the Trappist order appeals to me as a model of wisdom. By two in the morning the clapper goes upon the bell, and so on, hour by hour, and sometimes quarter by quarter, till eight, the hour of rest; so infinitesimally is the day divided among different occupations. The man who keeps rabbits, for example, hurries from his hutches to the chapel, the chapter-room, or the refectory, all day long: every hour he has an office to sing, a duty to perform; from two, when he rises in the dark, till eight, when he returns to receive the comfortable gift

48

of sleep, he is upon his feet and occupied with manifold and changing business. I know many persons, worth several thousands in the year, who are not so fortunate in the disposal of their lives. Into how many houses would not the note of the monastery bell, dividing the day into manageable portions, bring peace of mind and healthful activity of body! We speak of hardships, but the true hardship is to be a dull fool, and permitted to mismanage life in our own dull and foolish manner.

From this point of view, we may perhaps better understand the monk's existence. A long novitiate and every proof of constancy of mind and strength of body is required before admission to the order; but I could not find that many were discouraged.

In the photographer's studio, which figures so strangely among the outbuildings, my eye was attracted by the portrait of a young fellow in the uniform of a private of foot. This was one of the novices, who came of the age for service, and marched and drilled and mounted guard for the proper time among the garrison of Algiers. Here was a man who had surely seen both sides of life before deciding; yet as soon as he was set free from service he returned to finish his novitiate.

This austere rule entitles a man to heaven as by right. When the Trappist sickens, he quits not his habit; he lies in the bed of death as he has prayed and laboured in his frugal and silent existence; and when the Liberator comes, at the very moment, even before they have carried him in his robe to lie his little last in the chapel among continual chantings, joy-bells break forth, as if for a marriage, from the slated belfry, and proclaim throughout the neighbourhood that another soul has gone to God.

At night, under the conduct of my kind Irishman, I took my place in the gallery to hear compline and Salve Regina, with which the Cistercians bring every day to a conclusion. There were none of those circumstances which strike the Protestant as childish or as tawdry in the public offices of Rome. A stern simplicity, heightened by the romance of the surroundings, spoke directly to the heart. I recall the whitewashed chapel, the hooded figures in the choir, the lights alternately occluded and revealed, the strong manly singing, the silence that ensued, the sight of cowled heads bowed in prayer, and then the clear trenchant beating of the bell, breaking in to show that the last office was over and the hour of sleep had come; and when I remember, I am not surprised that I made my escape into the court with somewhat whirling fancies, and stood like a man bewildered in the windy starry night.

But I was weary; and when I had quieted my spirits with Elizabeth Seton's memoirs - a dull work - the cold and the raving of the wind among the pines (for my room was on that side of the monastery which adjoins the woods) disposed me readily to slumber. I was wakened at black midnight, as it seemed, though it was really two in the morning, by the first stroke upon the bell. All the brothers were then hurrying to the chapel; the dead in life, at this untimely hour, were already beginning the uncomforted labours of their day. The dead in life - there was a chill reflection. And the words of a French song came back into my memory, telling of the best of our mixed existence:

'Que t'as de belles filles,
  Girofle!
  Girofla!
Que t'as de belles filles,
L'Amour let comptera!'

And I blessed God that I was free to wander, free to hope, and free to love.

Chapter Eight

The boarders

BUT THERE WAS ANOTHER side to my residence at Our Lady of the Snows. At this late season there were not many boarders; and yet I was not alone in the public part of the monastery. This itself is hard by the gate, with a small dining-room on the ground-floor and a whole corridor of cells similar to mine upstairs. I have stupidly forgotten the board for a regular retraitant; but it was somewhere between three and five francs a day, and I think most probably the first. Chance visitors like myself might give what they chose as a free-will offering, but nothing was demanded. I may mention that when I was going away, Father Michael refused twenty francs as excessive. I explained the reasoning which led me to offer him so much; but even then, from a curious point of honour, he would not accept it with his own hand. 'I have no right to refuse for the monastery,' he explained, 'but I should prefer if you would give it to one of the brothers.'

I had dined alone, because I arrived late; but at supper I found two other guests. One was a country parish priest, who had walked over that morning from the seat of his cure near Mende to enjoy four days of solitude and prayer. He was a grenadier in person, with the hale colour and circular wrinkles of a peasant; and as he complained much of how he had been impeded by his skirts upon the march, I have a vivid fancy portrait of him, striding along, upright, big-boned, with kilted cassock, through the bleak hills of Gevaudan. The other was a short, grizzling, thick-set man, from forty-five to fifty, dressed in tweed with a knitted spencer, and the red ribbon of a decoration in his button-hole. This last was a hard person to classify. He was an old soldier, who had seen service and risen to the rank of commandant; and he retained some of the brisk decisive manners of the camp. On the other hand, as soon as his resignation was accepted, he had come to Our Lady of the Snows as a boarder, and, after a brief experience of its ways, had decided to remain as a novice. Already the new life was beginning to modify his appearance; already he had acquired somewhat of the quiet and smiling air of the brethren; and he was as yet neither an officer nor a Trappist, but partook of the character of each. And certainly here was a man in an interesting nick of life. Out of the noise of cannon and trumpets, he was in the act of passing into this still country bordering on the grave, where men sleep nightly in their grave-clothes, and, like phantoms, communicate by signs.

At supper we talked politics. I make it my business, when I am in France, to preach political good-will and moderation, and to dwell on the example of Poland, much as some alarmists in England dwell on the example of Carthage. The priest and the commandant assured me of their sympathy with all I said, and made a heavy sighing over the bitterness of contemporary feeling.

'Why, you cannot say anything to a man with which he does not absolutely agree,' said I, 'but he flies up at you in a temper.'

They both declared that such a state of things was antichristian. While we were thus agreeing, what should my tongue stumble upon but a word in praise of Gambetta's moderation. The old soldier's countenance was instantly suffused with blood; with the palms of his hands he beat the table like a naughty child.

'Comment, monsieur?' he shouted. 'Comment? Gambetta moderate? Will you dare to justify these words?'

But the priest had not forgotten the tenor of our talk. And suddenly, in the height of his fury, the old soldier found a warning look directed on his face; the absurdity of his behaviour was brought home to him in a flash; and the storm came to an abrupt end, without another word.

It was only in the morning, over our coffee (Friday, September 27th), that this couple found out I was a heretic. I suppose I had misled them by some admiring expressions as to the monastic life around us; and it was only by a point-blank question that the truth came out. I had been tolerantly used both by simple Father Apollinaris and astute Father Michael; and the good Irish deacon, when he heard of my religious weakness, had only patted me upon the shoulder and said, 'You must be a Catholic and come to heaven.' But I was now among a different sect of orthodox. These two men were bitter and upright and narrow, like the worst of Scotsmen, and indeed, upon my heart, I fancy they were worse. The priest snorted aloud like a battle-horse.

'Et vous pretendez mourir dans cette espece de croyance?' he demanded; and there is no type used by mortal printers large enough to qualify his accent.

I humbly indicated that I had no design of changing.

But he could not away with such a monstrous attitude. 'No, no,' he cried; 'you must change. You have come here, God has led you here, and you must embrace the opportunity.'

I made a slip in policy; I appealed to the family affections, though I was speaking to a priest and a soldier, two classes of men circumstantially divorced from the kind and homely ties of life.

'Your father and mother?' cried the priest. 'Very well; you will convert them in their turn when you go home.'

I think I see my father's face! I would rather tackle the Gaetulian lion in his den than embark on such an enterprise against the family theologian.

But now the hunt was up; priest and soldier were in full cry for my conversion; and the Work of the Propagation of the Faith, for which the people of Cheylard subscribed forty-eight francs ten centimes during 1877, was being gallantly pursued against myself. It was an odd but most effective proselytising. They never sought to convince me in argument, where I might have attempted some defence; but took it for granted that I was both ashamed and terrified at my position, and urged me solely on the point of time. Now, they said, when God had led me to Our Lady of the Snows, now was the appointed hour.

'Do not be withheld by false shame,' observed the priest, for my encouragement. For one who feels very similarly to all sects of religion, and who has never been able, even for a moment, to weigh seriously the merit of this or that creed on the eternal side of things, however much he may see to praise or blame upon the secular and temporal side, the situation thus created was both unfair and painful. I committed my second fault in tact, and tried to plead that it was all the same thing in the end, and we were all drawing near by different sides to the same kind and undiscriminating Friend and Father. That, as it seems to lay spirits, would be the only gospel worthy of the name. But different men think differently; and this revolutionary aspiration brought down the priest with all the terrors of the law. He launched into harrowing details of hell. The damned, he said - on the authority of a little book which he had read not a week before, and which, to add conviction to conviction, he had fully intended to bring along with him in his pocket - were to occupy the same attitude through all eternity in the midst of dismal tortures. And as he thus expatiated, he grew in nobility of aspect with his enthusiasm.

As a result the pair concluded that I should seek out the Prior, since the Abbot was from home, and lay my case immediately before him.

'C'est mon conseil comme ancien militaire,' observed the commandant; 'et celui de monsieur comme pretre.'

Oui,' added the cure, sententiously nodding; 'comme ancien militaire—et comme pretre.'

At this moment, whilst I was somewhat embarrassed how to answer, in came one of the monks, a little brown fellow, as lively as a grig, and with an Italian accent, who threw himself at once into the contention, but in a milder and more persuasive vein, as befitted one of these pleasant brethren. Look at him, he said. The rule was very hard; he would have dearly liked to stay in his own country, Italy - it was well known how beautiful it was, the beautiful Italy; but then there were no Trappists in Italy; and he had a soul to save; and here he was.

I am afraid I must be at bottom, what a cheerful Indian critic has dubbed me, 'a faddling hedonist,' for this description of the brother's motives gave me somewhat of a shock. I should have preferred to think he had chosen the life for its own sake, and not for ulterior purposes; and this shows how profoundly I was out of sympathy with these good Trappists, even when I was doing my best to sympathise. But to the cure the argument seemed decisive.

'Hear that!' he cried. 'And I have seen a marquis here, a marquis, a marquis' - he repeated the holy word three times over - 'and other persons high in society; and generals. And here, at your side, is this gentleman, who has been so many years in armies - decorated, an old warrior. And here he is, ready to dedicate himself to God.'

I was by this time so thoroughly embarrassed that I pled cold feet, and made my escape from the apartment. It was a furious windy morning, with a sky much cleared, and long and potent intervals of sunshine; and I wandered until dinner in the wild country towards the east, sorely staggered and beaten upon by the gale, but rewarded with some striking views.

At dinner the Work of the Propagation of the Faith was recommenced, and on this occasion still more distastefully to me. The priest asked me many questions as to the contemptible faith of my fathers, and received my replies with a kind of ecclesiastical titter.

'Your sect,' he said once; 'for I think you will admit it would be doing it too much honour to call it a religion.'

'As you please, monsieur,' said I. 'La parole est a vous.'

At length I grew annoyed beyond endurance; and although he was on his own ground and, what is more to the purpose, an old man, and so holding a claim upon my toleration, I could not avoid a protest against this uncivil usage. He was sadly discountenanced.

'I assure you,' he said, 'I have no inclination to laugh in my heart. I have no other feeling but interest in your soul.'

And there ended my conversion. Honest man! he was no dangerous deceiver; but a country parson, full of zeal and faith. Long may he tread Gevaudan with his kilted skirts - a man strong to walk and strong to comfort his parishioners in death! I daresay he would beat bravely through a snowstorm where his duty called him; and it is not always the most faithful believer who makes the cunningest apostle.

Upper Gevaudan

(continued)

The bed was made, the room was fit,
By punctual eve the stars were lit;
The air was still, the water ran;
No need there was for maid or man,
When we put up, my ass and I,
At God's green caravanserai.

OLD PLAY

Chapter Nine

Across the Goulet

THE WIND FELL during dinner, and the sky remained clear; so it was under better auspices that I loaded Modestine before the monastery gate. My Irish friend accompanied me so far on the way. As we came through the wood, there was Pere Apollinaire hauling his barrow; and he too quitted his labours to go with me for perhaps a hundred yards, holding my hand between both of his in front of him. I parted first from one and then from the other with unfeigned regret, but yet with the glee of the traveller who shakes off the dust of one stage before hurrying forth upon another. Then Modestine and I mounted the course of the Allier, which here led us back into Gevaudan towards its sources in the forest of Mercoire. It was but an inconsiderable burn before we left its guidance. Thence, over a hill, our way lay through a naked plateau, until we reached Chasserades at sundown.

The company in the inn kitchen that night were all men employed in survey for one of the projected railways. They were intelligent and conversible, and we decided the future of France over hot wine, until the state of the clock frightened us to rest. There were four beds in the little upstairs room; and we slept six. But I had a bed to myself, and persuaded them to leave the window open.

'He, bourgeois; il est cinq heures!' was the cry that wakened me in the morning (Saturday, September 28th). The room was full of a transparent darkness, which dimly showed me the other three beds and the five different nightcaps on the pillows. But out of the window the dawn was growing ruddy in a long belt over the hill-tops, and day was about to flood the plateau. The hour was inspiriting; and there seemed a promise of calm weather, which was perfectly fulfilled. I was soon under way with Modestine. The road lay for a while over the plateau, and then descended through a precipitous village into the valley of the Chassezac. This stream ran among green meadows, well hidden from the world by its steep banks; the broom was in flower, and here and there was a hamlet sending up its smoke.

At last the path crossed the Chassezac upon a bridge, and, forsaking this deep hollow, set itself to cross the mountain of La Goulet. It wound up through Lestampes by upland fields and woods of beech and birch, and with every corner brought me into an acquaintance with some new interest. Even in the gully of the Chassezac my ear had been struck by a noise like that of a great bass bell ringing at the distance of many miles; but this, as I continued to mount and draw nearer to it, seemed to change in character, and I found at length that it came from some one leading flocks afield to the note of a rural horn. The narrow street of Lestampes stood full of sheep, from wall to wall - black sheep and white, bleating with one accord like the birds in spring, and each one accompanying himself upon the sheep-bell round his neck. It made a pathetic concert, all in treble. A little higher, and I passed a pair of men in a tree with pruning-hooks, and one of them was singing the music of a bourree. Still further, and when I was already threading the birches, the crowing of cocks came cheerfully up to my ears, and along with that the voice of a flute discoursing a deliberate and plaintive air from one of the upland villages. I pictured to myself some grizzled, apple-cheeked, country schoolmaster fluting in his bit of a garden in the clear autumn sunshine. All these beautiful and interesting sounds filled my heart with an unwonted expectation; and it appeared to me that, once past this range which I was mounting, I should descend into the garden of the world. Nor was I deceived, for I was now done with rains and winds and a bleak country. The first part of my journey ended here; and this was like an induction of sweet sounds into the other and more beautiful.

There are other degrees of feyness, as of punishment, besides the capital; and I was now led by my good spirits into an adventure which I relate in the interest of future donkey-drivers. The road zigzagged so widely on the hillside that I chose a short cut by map and compass, and struck through the dwarf woods to catch the road again upon a higher level. It was my one serious conflict with Modestine. She would none of my short cut; she turned in my face; she backed, she reared; she, whom I had hitherto imagined to be dumb, actually brayed with a loud hoarse flourish, like a cock crowing for the dawn. I plied the goad with one hand; with the other, so steep was the ascent, I had to hold on the pack-saddle. Half-a-dozen times she was nearly over backwards on the top of me; half-a-dozen times, from sheer weariness of spirit, I was nearly giving it up, and leading her down again to follow the road. But I took the thing as a wager, and fought it through. I was surprised, as I went on my way again, by what appeared to be chill rain-drops falling on my hand, and more than once looked up in wonder at the cloudless sky. But it was only sweat which came dropping from my brow.

Over the summit of the Goulet there was no marked road - only upright stones posted from space to space to guide the drovers. The turf underfoot was springy and well scented. I had no company but a lark or two, and met but one bullock-cart between Lestampes and Bleymard. In front of me I saw a shallow valley, and beyond that the range of the Lozere, sparsely wooded and well enough modelled in the flanks, but straight and dull in outline. There was scarce a sign of culture; only about Bleymard, the white high-road from Villefort to Mende traversed a range of meadows, set with spiry poplars, and sounding from side to side with the bells of flocks and herds.

"Among the pines" - frontispiece to the original 1879 edition

Chapter Ten

A night among the pines

F ROM BLEYMARD after dinner, although it was already late, I set out to scale a portion of the Lozere. An ill-marked stony drove-road guided me forward; and I met nearly half-a-dozen bullock-carts descending from the woods, each laden with a whole pine-tree for the winter's firing. At the top of the woods, which do not climb very high upon this cold ridge, I struck leftward by a path among the pines, until I hit on a dell of green turf, where a streamlet made a little spout over some stones to serve me for a water-tap. 'In a more sacred or sequestered bower . . . nor nymph nor faunus haunted.' The trees were not old, but they grew thickly round the glade: there was no outlook, except north-eastward upon distant hill-tops, or straight upward to the sky; and the encampment felt secure and private like a room. By the time I had made my arrangements and fed Modestine, the day was already beginning to decline. I buckled myself to the knees into my sack and made a hearty meal; and as soon as the sun went down, I pulled my cap over my eyes and fell asleep.

Night is a dead monotonous period under a roof; but in the open world it passes lightly, with its stars and dews and perfumes, and the hours are marked by changes in the face of Nature. What seems a kind of temporal death to people choked between walls and curtains, is only a light and living slumber to the man who sleeps afield. All night long he can hear Nature breathing deeply and freely; even as she takes her rest, she turns and smiles; and there is one stirring hour unknown to those who dwell in houses, when a wakeful influence goes abroad over the sleeping hemisphere, and all the outdoor world are on their feet.

It is then that the cock first crows, not this time to announce the dawn, but like a cheerful watchman speeding the course of night. Cattle awake on the meadows; sheep break their fast on dewy hillsides, and change to a new lair among the ferns; and houseless men, who have lain down with the fowls, open their dim eyes and behold the beauty of the night.

At what inaudible summons, at what gentle touch of Nature, are all these sleepers thus recalled in the same hour to life? Do the stars rain down an influence, or do we share some thrill of mother earth below our resting bodies? Even shepherds and old country-folk, who are the deepest read in these arcana, have not a guess as to the means or purpose of this nightly resurrection. Towards two in the morning they declare the thing takes place; and neither know nor inquire further. And at least it is a pleasant incident. We are disturbed in our slumber only, like the luxurious Montaigne, 'that we may the better and more sensibly relish it.' We have a moment to look upon the stars. And there is a special pleasure for some minds in the reflection that we share the impulse with all outdoor creatures in our neighbourhood, that we have escaped out of the Bastille of civilisation, and are become, for the time being, a mere kindly animal and a sheep of Nature's flock.

When that hour came to me among the pines, I wakened thirsty. My tin was standing by me half full of water. I emptied it at a draught; and feeling broad awake after this internal cold aspersion, sat upright to make a cigarette. The stars were clear, coloured, and jewel-like, but not frosty. A faint silvery vapour stood for the Milky Way. All around me the black fir-points stood upright and stock-still. By the whiteness of the pack-saddle, I could see Modestine walking round and round at the length of her tether; I could hear her steadily munching at the sward; but there was not another sound, save the indescribable quiet talk of the runnel over the stones. I lay lazily smoking and studying the colour of the sky, as we call the void of space, from where it showed a reddish grey behind the pines to where it showed a glossy blue-black between the stars. As if to be more like a pedlar, I wear a silver ring. This I could see faintly shining as I raised or lowered the cigarette; and at each whiff the inside of my hand was illuminated, and became for a second the highest light in the landscape.

A faint wind, more like a moving coolness than a stream of air, passed down the glade from time to time; so that even in my great chamber the air was being renewed all night long. I thought with horror of the inn at Chasserades and the congregated nightcaps; with horror of the nocturnal prowesses of clerks and students, of hot theatres and pass-keys and close rooms. I have not often enjoyed a more serene possession of myself, nor felt more independent of material aids. The outer world, from which we cower into our houses, seemed after all a gentle habitable place; and night after night a man's bed, it seemed, was laid and waiting for him in the fields, where God keeps an open house. I thought I had rediscovered one of those truths which are revealed to savages and hid from political economists: at the least, I had discovered a new pleasure for myself. And yet even while I was exulting in my solitude I became aware of a strange lack. I wished a companion to lie near me in the starlight, silent and not moving, but ever within touch. For there is a fellowship more quiet even than solitude, and which, rightly understood, is solitude made perfect. And to live out of doors with the woman a man loves is of all lives the most complete and free.

As I thus lay, between content and longing, a faint noise stole towards me through the pines. I thought, at first, it was the crowing of cocks or the barking of dogs at some very distant farm; but steadily and gradually it took articulate shape in my ears, until I became aware that a passenger was going by upon the high-road in the valley, and singing loudly as he went. There was more of good-will than grace in his performance; but he trolled with ample lungs; and the sound of his voice took hold upon the hillside and set the air shaking in the leafy glens. I have heard people passing by night in sleeping cities; some of them sang; one, I remember, played loudly on the bagpipes. I have heard the rattle of a cart or carriage spring up suddenly after hours of stillness, and pass, for some minutes, within the range of my hearing as I lay abed. There is a romance about all who are abroad in the black hours, and with something of a thrill we try to guess their business. But here the romance was double: first, this glad passenger, lit internally with wine, who sent up his voice in music through the night; and then I, on the other hand, buckled into my sack, and smoking alone in the pine-woods between four and five thousand feet towards the stars.

When I awoke again (Sunday, 29th September), many of the stars had disappeared; only the stronger companions of the night still burned visibly overhead; and away towards the east I saw a faint haze of light upon the horizon, such as had been the Milky Way when I was last awake. Day was at hand. I lit my lantern, and by its glow-worm light put on my boots and gaiters; then I broke up some bread for Modestine, filled my can at the water-tap, and lit my spirit-lamp to boil myself some chocolate. The blue darkness lay long in the glade where I had so sweetly slumbered; but soon there was a broad streak of orange melting into gold along the mountain-tops of Vivarais. A solemn glee possessed my mind at this gradual and lovely coming in of day. I heard the runnel with delight; I looked round me for something beautiful and unexpected; but the still black pine-trees, the hollow glade, the munching ass, remained unchanged in figure. Nothing had altered but the light, and that, indeed, shed over all a spirit of life and of breathing peace, and moved me to a strange exhilaration.

I drank my water-chocolate, which was hot if it was not rich, and strolled here and there, and up and down about the glade. While I was thus delaying, a gush of steady wind, as long as a heavy sigh, poured direct out of the quarter of the morning. It was cold, and set me sneezing. The trees near at hand tossed their black plumes in its passage; and I could see the thin distant spires of pine along the edge of the hill rock slightly to and fro against the golden east. Ten minutes after, the sunlight spread at a gallop along the hillside, scattering shadows and sparkles, and the day had come completely.

I hastened to prepare my pack, and tackle the steep ascent that lay before me; but I had something on my mind. It was only a fancy; yet a fancy will sometimes be importunate. I had been most hospitably received and punctually served in my green caravanserai. The room was airy, the water excellent, and the dawn had called me to a moment. I say nothing of the tapestries or the inimitable ceiling, nor yet of the view which I commanded from the windows; but I felt I was in some one's debt for all this liberal entertainment. And so it pleased me, in a half-laughing way, to leave pieces of money on the turf as I went along, until I had left enough for my night's lodging. I trust they did not fall to some rich and churlish drover.

"The sunlight spread at a gallop along the hillside, scattering shadows and sparkles"

65

The Country of the Camisards

We travelled in the print of olden wars;
    Yet all the land was green;
    And love we found, and peace,
    Where fire and war had been.
They pass and smile, the children of the sword -
    No more the sword they wield;
    And O, how deep the corn
    Along the battlefield!

W. P. BANNATYNE

Chapter Eleven

Across the Lozere

THE TRACK THAT I had followed in the evening soon died out, and I continued to follow over a bald turf ascent a row of stone pillars, such as had conducted me across the Goulet. It was already warm. I tied my jacket on the pack, and walked in my knitted waistcoat. Modestine herself was in high spirits, and broke of her own accord, for the first time in my experience, into a jolting trot that set the oats swashing in the pocket of my coat. The view, back upon the northern Gevaudan, extended with every step; scarce a tree, scarce a house, appeared upon the fields of wild hill that ran north, east, and west, all blue and gold in the haze and sunlight of the morning. A multitude of little birds kept sweeping and twittering about my path; they perched on the stone pillar, they pecked and strutted on the turf, and I saw them circle in volleys in the blue air, and show, from time to time, translucent flickering wings between the sun and me.

Almost from the first moment of my march, a faint large noise, like a distant surf, had filled my ears. Sometimes I was tempted to think it the voice of a neighbouring waterfall, and sometimes a subjective result of the utter stillness of the hill. But as I continued to advance, the noise increased, and became like the hissing of an enormous tea-urn, and at the same time breaths of cool air began to reach me from the direction of the summit. At length I understood. It was blowing stiffly from the south upon the other slope of the Lozere, and every step that I took I was drawing nearer to the wind.

Although it had been long desired, it was quite unexpectedly at last that my eyes rose above the summit. A step that seemed no way more decisive than many other steps that had preceded it - and, 'like stout Cortez when, with eagle eyes, he stared on the Pacific,' I took possession, in my own name, of a new quarter of the world. For behold, instead of the gross turf rampart I had been mounting for so long, a view into the hazy air of heaven, and a land of intricate blue hills below my feet.

The Lozere lies nearly east and west, cutting Gevaudan into two unequal parts; its highest point, this Pic de Finiels, on which I was then standing, rises upwards of five thousand six hundred feet above the sea, and in clear weather commands a view over all lower Languedoc to the Mediterranean Sea. I have spoken with people who either pretended or believed that they had seen, from the Pic de Finiels, white ships sailing by Montpellier and Cette. Behind was the upland northern country through which my way had lain, peopled by a dull race, without wood, without much grandeur of hill-form, and famous in the past for little beside wolves. But in front of me, half veiled in sunny haze, lay a new Gevaudan, rich, picturesque, illustrious for stirring events.

Speaking largely, I was in the Cevennes at Monastier, and during all my journey; but there is a strict and local sense in which only this confused and shaggy country at my feet has any title to the name, and in this sense the peasantry employ the word. These are the Cevennes with an emphasis: the Cevennes of the Cevennes. In that undecipherable labyrinth of hills, a war of bandits, a war of wild beasts, raged for two years between the Grand Monarch with all his troops and marshals on the one hand, and a few thousand Protestant mountaineers upon the other. A hundred and eighty years ago, the Camisards held a station even on the Lozere, where I stood; they had an organisation, arsenals, a military and religious hierarchy; their affairs were 'the discourse of every coffee-house' in London; England sent fleets in their support; their leaders prophesied and murdered; with colours and drums, and the singing of old French psalms, their bands sometimes affronted daylight, marched before walled cities, and dispersed the generals of the king; and sometimes at night, or in masquerade, possessed themselves of strong castles, and avenged treachery upon their allies and cruelty upon their foes. There, a hundred and eighty years ago, was the chivalrous Roland, 'Count and Lord Roland, generalissimo of the Protestants in France,' grave, silent, imperious, pockmarked ex-dragoon, whom a lady followed in his wanderings out of love. There was Cavalier, a baker's apprentice with a genius for war, elected brigadier of Camisards at seventeen, to die at fifty-five the English governor of Jersey. There again was Castanet, a partisan leader in a voluminous peruke and with a taste for controversial divinity. Strange generals, who moved apart to take counsel with the God of Hosts, and fled or offered battle, set sentinels or slept in an unguarded camp, as the Spirit whispered to their hearts! And there, to follow these and other leaders, was the rank and file of prophets and disciples, bold, patient, indefatigable, hardy to run upon the mountains, cheering their rough life with psalms, eager to fight, eager to pray, listening devoutly to the oracles of brain-sick children, and mystically putting a grain of wheat among the pewter balls with which they charged their muskets.

I had travelled hitherto through a dull district, and in the track of nothing more notable than the child-eating beast of Gevaudan, the Napoleon Bonaparte of wolves. But now I was to go down into the scene of a romantic chapter - or, better, a romantic footnote in the history of the world. What was left of all this bygone dust and heroism? I was told that Protestantism still survived in this head seat of Protestant resistance; so much the priest himself had told me in the monastery parlour. But I had yet to learn if it were a bare survival, or a lively and generous tradition. Again, if in the northern Cevennes the people are narrow in religious judgments, and more filled with zeal than charity, what was I to look for in this land of persecution and reprisal - in a land where the tyranny of the Church produced the Camisard rebellion, and the terror of the Camisards threw the Catholic peasantry into legalised revolt upon the other side, so that Camisard and Florentin skulked for each other's lives among the mountains?

Just on the brow of the hill, where I paused to look before me, the series of stone pillars came abruptly to an end; and only a little below, a sort of track appeared and began to go down a break-neck slope, turning like a corkscrew as it went. It led into a valley between falling hills, stubbly with rocks like a reaped field of corn, and floored farther down with green meadows. I followed the track with precipitation; the steepness of the slope, the continual agile turning of the line of the descent, and the old unwearied hope of finding something new in a new country, all conspired to lend me wings. Yet a little lower and a stream began, collecting itself together out of many fountains, and soon making a glad noise among the hills. Sometimes it would cross the track in a bit of waterfall, with a pool, in which Modestine refreshed her feet.

The whole descent is like a dream to me, so rapidly was it accomplished. I had scarcely left the summit ere the valley had closed round my path, and the sun beat upon me, walking in a stagnant lowland atmosphere. The track became a road, and went up and down in easy undulations. I passed cabin after cabin, but all seemed deserted; and I saw not a human creature, nor heard any sound except that of the stream. I was, however, in a different country from the day before. The stony skeleton of the world was here vigorously displayed to sun and air. The slopes were steep and changeful. Oak-trees clung along the hills, well grown, wealthy in leaf, and touched by the autumn with strong and luminous colours. Here and there another stream would fall in from the right or the left, down a gorge of snow-white and tumultuary boulders. The river in the bottom (for it was rapidly growing a river, collecting on all hands as it trotted on its way) here foamed a while in desperate rapids, and there lay in pools of the most enchanting sea-green shot with watery browns. As far as I have gone, I have never seen a river of so changeful and delicate a hue; crystal was not more clear, the meadows were not by half so green; and at every pool I saw I felt a thrill of longing to be out of these hot, dusty, and material garments, and bathe my naked body in the mountain air and water. All the time as I went on I never forgot it was the Sabbath; the stillness was a perpetual reminder; and I heard in spirit the church-bells clamouring all over Europe, and the psalms of a thousand churches.

At length a human sound struck upon my ear - a cry strangely modulated between pathos and derision; and looking across the valley, I saw a little urchin sitting in a meadow, with his hands about his knees, and dwarfed to almost comical smallness by the distance. But the rogue had picked me out as I went down the road, from oak wood on to oak wood, driving Modestine; and he made me the compliments of the new country in this tremulous high-pitched salutation. And as all noises are lovely and natural at a sufficient distance, this also, coming through so much clean hill air and crossing all the green valley, sounded pleasant to my ear, and seemed a thing rustic, like the oaks or the river.

A little after, the stream that I was following fell into the Tarn at Pont de Montvert of bloody memory.

Chapter Twelve

Pont de Montvert

O NE OF THE FIRST things I encountered in Pont de Montvert was, if I remember rightly, the Protestant temple; but this was but the type of other novelties. A subtle atmosphere distinguishes a town in England from a town in France, or even in Scotland. At Carlisle you can see you are in the one country; at Dumfries, thirty miles away, you are as sure that you are in the other. I should find it difficult to tell in what particulars Pont de Montvert differed from Monastier or Langogne, or even Bleymard; but the difference existed, and spoke eloquently to the eyes. The place, with its houses, its lanes, its glaring river-bed, wore an indescribable air of the South.

All was Sunday bustle in the streets and in the public-house, as all had been Sabbath peace among the mountains. There must have been near a score of us at dinner by eleven before noon; and after I had eaten and drunken, and sat writing up my journal, I suppose as many more came dropping in one after another, or by twos and threes.

In crossing the Lozere I had not only come among new natural features, but moved into the territory of a different race. These people, as they hurriedly despatched their viands in an intricate sword-play of knives, questioned and answered me with a degree of intelligence which excelled all that I had met, except among the railway folk at Chasserades.

They had open telling faces, and were lively both in speech and manner. They not only entered thoroughly into the spirit of my little trip, but more than one declared, if he were rich enough, he would like to set forth on such another.

Even physically there was a pleasant change. I had not seen a pretty woman since I left Monastier, and there but one. Now of the three who sat down with me to dinner, one was certainly not beautiful - a poor timid thing of forty, quite troubled at this roaring table d'hôte, whom I squired and helped to wine, and pledged and tried generally to encourage, with quite a contrary effect; but the other two, both married, were both more handsome than the average of women.

And Clarisse? What shall I say of Clarisse? She waited the table with a heavy placable nonchalance, like a performing cow; her great grey eyes were steeped in amorous languor; her features, although fleshy, were of an original and accurate design; her mouth had a curl; her nostril spoke of dainty pride; her cheek fell into strange and interesting lines. It was a face capable of strong emotion, and, with training, it offered the promise of delicate sentiment. It seemed pitiful to see so good a model left to country admirers and a country way of thought. Beauty should at least have touched society; then, in a moment, it throws off a weight that lay upon it, it becomes conscious of itself, it puts on an elegance, learns a gait and a carriage of the head, and, in a moment, patet dea. Before I left I assured Clarisse of my hearty admiration. She took it like milk, without embarrassment or wonder, merely looking at me steadily with her great eyes; and I own the result upon myself was some confusion. If Clarisse could read English, I should not dare to add that her figure was unworthy of her face. Hers was a case for stays; but that may perhaps grow better as she gets up in years.

Pont de Montvert, or Greenhill Bridge, as we might say at home, is a place memorable in the story of the Camisards. It was here that the war broke out; here that those southern Covenanters slew their Archbishop Sharp. The persecution on the one hand, the febrile enthusiasm on the other, are almost equally difficult to understand in these quiet modern days, and with our easy modern beliefs and disbeliefs. The Protestants were one and all beside their right minds with zeal and sorrow. They were all prophets and prophetesses. Children at the breast would exhort their parents to good works. 'A child of fifteen months at Quissac spoke from its mother's arms, agitated and sobbing, distinctly and with a loud voice.' Marshal Villars has seen a town where all the women 'seemed possessed by the devil,' and had trembling fits, and uttered prophecies publicly upon the streets. A prophetess of Vivarais was hanged at Montpellier because blood flowed from her eyes and nose, and she declared that she was weeping tears of blood for the misfortunes of the Protestants. And it was not only women and children. Stalwart dangerous fellows, used to swing the sickle or to wield the forest axe, were likewise shaken with strange paroxysms, and spoke oracles with sobs and streaming tears. A persecution unsurpassed in violence had lasted near a score of years, and this was the result upon the persecuted; hanging, burning, breaking on the wheel, had been in vain; the dragoons had left their hoof-marks over all the countryside; there were men rowing in the galleys, and women pining in the prisons of the Church; and not a thought was changed in the heart of any upright Protestant.

Now the head and forefront of the persecution - after Lamoignon de Bavile - Francois de Langlade du Chayla (pronounce Cheila), Archpriest of the Cevennes and Inspector of Missions in the same country, had a house in which he sometimes dwelt in the town of Pont de Montvert. He was a conscientious person, who seems to have been intended by nature for a pirate, and now fifty-five, an age by which a man has learned all the moderation of which he is capable. A missionary in his youth in China, he there suffered martyrdom, was left for dead, and only succoured and brought back to life by the charity of a pariah. We must suppose the pariah devoid of second-sight, and not purposely malicious in this act. Such an experience, it might be thought, would have cured a man of the desire to persecute; but the human spirit is a thing strangely put together; and, having been a Christian martyr, Du Chayla became a Christian persecutor. The Work of the Propagation of the Faith went roundly forward in his hands. His house in Pont de Montvert served him as a prison. There he closed the hands of his prisoners upon live coal, and plucked out the hairs of their beards, to convince them that they were deceived in their opinions. And yet had not he himself tried and proved the inefficacy of these carnal arguments among the Buddhists in China?

Not only was life made intolerable in Languedoc, but flight was rigidly forbidden. One Massip, a muleteer, and well acquainted with the mountain-paths, had already guided several troops of fugitives in safety to Geneva; and on him, with another convoy, consisting mostly of women dressed as men, Du Chayla, in an evil hour for himself, laid his hands. The Sunday following, there was a conventicle of Protestants in the woods of Altefage upon Mount Bouges; where there stood up one Seguier—Spirit Seguier, as his companions called him - a wool-carder, tall, black-faced, and toothless, but a man full of prophecy.

The house of Du Chayla ever stands by the bridge at Pont de Montvert.

He declared, in the name of God, that the time for submission had gone by, and they must betake themselves to arms for the deliverance of their brethren and the destruction of the priests.

The next night, 24th July 1702, a sound disturbed the Inspector of Missions as he sat in his prison-house at Pont de Montvert: the voices of many men upraised in psalmody drew nearer and nearer through the town. It was ten at night; he had his court about him, priests, soldiers, and servants, to the number of twelve or fifteen; and now dreading the insolence of a conventicle below his very windows, he ordered forth his soldiers to report. But the psalm-singers were already at his door, fifty strong, led by the inspired Seguier, and breathing death. To their summons, the archpriest made answer like a stout old persecutor, and bade his garrison fire upon the mob. One Camisard (for, according to some, it was in this night's work that they came by the name) fell at this discharge: his comrades burst in the door with hatchets and a beam of wood, overran the lower story of the house, set free the prisoners, and finding one of them in the vine, a sort of Scavenger's Daughter of the place and period, redoubled in fury against Du Chayla, and sought by repeated assaults to carry the upper floors. But he, on his side, had given absolution to his men, and they bravely held the staircase.

'Children of God,' cried the prophet, 'hold your hands. Let us burn the house, with the priest and the satellites of Baal.'
The fire caught readily. Out of an upper window Du Chayla and his men lowered themselves into the garden by means of knotted sheets; some escaped across the river under the bullets of the insurgents; but the archpriest himself fell, broke his thigh, and could only crawl into the hedge. What were his reflections as this second martyrdom drew near? A poor, brave, besotted, hateful man, who had done his duty resolutely according to his light both in the Cevennes and China. He found at least one telling word to say in his defence; for when the roof fell in and the upbursting flames discovered his retreat, and they came and dragged him to the public place of the town, raging and calling him damned - 'If I be damned,' said he, 'why should you also damn yourselves?'

Here was a good reason for the last; but in the course of his inspectorship he had given many stronger which all told in a contrary direction; and these he was now to hear. One by one, Seguier first, the Camisards drew near and stabbed him. 'This,' they said, 'is for my father broken on the wheel. This for my brother in the galleys. That for my mother or my sister imprisoned in your cursed convents.' Each gave his blow and his reason;

and then all kneeled and sang psalms around the body till the dawn. With the dawn, still singing, they defiled away towards Frugeres, farther up the Tarn, to pursue the work of vengeance, leaving Du Chayla's prison-house in ruins, and his body pierced with two-and-fifty wounds upon the public place.

'Tis a wild night's work, with its accompaniment of psalms; and it seems as if a psalm must always have a sound of threatening in that town upon the Tarn. But the story does not end, even so far as concerns Pont de Montvert, with the departure of the Camisards. The career of Seguier was brief and bloody. Two more priests and a whole family at Ladeveze, from the father to the servants, fell by his hand or by his orders; and yet he was but a day or two at large, and restrained all the time by the presence of the soldiery. Taken at length by a famous soldier of fortune, Captain Poul, he appeared unmoved before his judges.

'Your name?' they asked.

'Pierre Seguier.'

'Why are you called Spirit?'

'Because the Spirit of the Lord is with me.'

'Your domicile?'

'Lately in the desert, and soon in heaven.'

'Have you no remorse for your crimes?'

'I have committed none. My soul is like a garden full of shelter and of fountains.'

At Pont de Montvert, on the 12th of August, he had his right hand stricken from his body, and was burned alive. And his soul was like a garden? So perhaps was the soul of Du Chayla, the Christian martyr. And perhaps if you could read in my soul, or I could read in yours, our own composure might seem little less surprising.

Du Chayla's house still stands, with a new roof, beside one of the bridges of the town; and if you are curious you may see the terrace-garden into which he dropped.

76

Chapter Thirteen

In the Valley of the Tarn

A NEW ROAD leads from Pont de Montvert to Florac by the valley of the Tarn; a smooth sandy ledge, it runs about half-way between the summit of the cliffs and the river in the bottom of the valley; and I went in and out, as I followed it, from bays of shadow into promontories of afternoon sun. This was a pass like that of Killiecrankie; a deep turning gully in the hills, with the Tarn making a wonderful hoarse uproar far below, and craggy summits standing in the sunshine high above.

A thin fringe of ash-trees ran about the hill-tops, like ivy on a ruin; but on the lower slopes, and far up every glen, the Spanish chestnut-trees stood each four-square to heaven under its tented foliage. Some were planted, each on its own terrace no larger than a bed; some, trusting in their roots, found strength to grow and prosper and be straight and large upon the rapid slopes of the valley; others, where there was a margin to the river, stood marshalled in a line and mighty like cedars of Lebanon. Yet even where they grew most thickly they were not to be thought of as a wood, but as a herd of stalwart individuals; and the dome of each tree stood forth separate and large, and as it were a little hill, from among the domes of its companions. They gave forth a faint sweet perfume which pervaded the air of the afternoon; autumn had put tints of gold and tarnish in the green; and the sun so shone through and kindled the broad foliage, that each chestnut was relieved against another, not in shadow, but in light. A humble sketcher here laid down his pencil in despair.

I wish I could convey a notion of the growth of these noble trees; of how they strike out boughs like the oak, and trail sprays of drooping foliage like the willow; of how they stand on upright fluted columns like the pillars of a church; or like the olive, from the most shattered bole can put out smooth and youthful shoots, and begin a new life upon the ruins of the old. Thus they partake of the nature of many different trees; and even their prickly top-knots, seen near at hand against the sky, have a certain palm-like air that impresses the imagination. But their individuality, although compounded of so many elements, is but the richer and the more original. And to look down upon a level filled with these knolls of foliage, or to see a clan of old unconquerable chestnuts cluster 'like herded elephants' upon the spur of a mountain, is to rise to higher thoughts of the powers that are in Nature.

Between Modestine's laggard humour and the beauty of the scene, we made little progress all that afternoon; and at last finding the sun, although still far from setting, was already beginning to desert the narrow valley of the Tarn, I began to cast about for a place to camp in. This was not easy to find; the terraces were too narrow, and the ground, where it was unterraced, was usually too steep for a man to lie upon. I should have slipped all night, and awakened towards morning with my feet or my head in the river.

After perhaps a mile, I saw, some sixty feet above the road, a little plateau large enough to hold my sack, and securely parapeted by the trunk of an aged and enormous chestnut. Thither, with infinite trouble, I goaded and kicked the reluctant Modestine, and there I hastened to unload her. There was only room for myself upon the plateau, and I had to go nearly as high again before I found so much as standing-room for the ass. It was on a heap of rolling stones, on an artificial terrace, certainly not five feet square in all. Here I tied her to a chestnut, and having given her corn and bread and made a pile of chestnut-leaves, of which I found her greedy, I descended once more to my own encampment.

The position was unpleasantly exposed. One or two carts went by upon the road; and as long as daylight lasted I concealed myself, for all the world like a hunted Camisard, behind my fortification of vast chestnut trunk; for I was passionately afraid of discovery and the visit of jocular persons in the night. Moreover, I saw that I must be early awake; for these chestnut gardens had been the scene of industry no further gone than on the day before. The slope was strewn with lopped branches, and here and there a great package of leaves was propped against a trunk; for even the leaves are serviceable, and the peasants use them in winter by way of fodder for their animals. I picked a meal in fear and trembling, half lying down to hide myself from the road; and I daresay I was as much concerned as if I had been a scout from Joani's band above upon the Lozere, or from Salomon's across the Tarn, in the old times of psalm-singing and blood. Or, indeed, perhaps more; for the Camisards had a remarkable confidence in God; and a tale comes back into my memory of how the Count of Gevaudan, riding with a party of dragoons and a notary at his saddlebow to enforce the oath of fidelity in all the country hamlets, entered a valley in the woods, and found Cavalier and his men at dinner, gaily seated on the grass, and their hats crowned with box-tree garlands, while fifteen women washed their linen in the stream. Such was a field festival in 1703; at that date Antony Watteau would be painting similar subjects.

This was a very different camp from that of the night before in the cool and silent pine-woods. It was warm and even stifling in the valley. The shrill song of frogs, like the tremolo note of a whistle with a pea in it, rang up from the river-side before the sun was down. In the growing dusk, faint rustlings began to run to and fro among the fallen leaves; from time to time a faint chirping or cheeping noise would fall upon my ear; and from time to time I thought I could see the movement of something swift and indistinct between the chestnuts. A profusion of large ants swarmed upon the ground; bats whisked by, and mosquitoes droned overhead. The long boughs with their bunches of leaves hung against the sky like garlands; and those immediately above and around me had somewhat the air of a trellis which should have been wrecked and half overthrown in a gale of wind.

Sleep for a long time fled my eyelids; and just as I was beginning to feel quiet stealing over my limbs, and settling densely on my mind, a noise at my head startled me broad awake again, and, I will frankly confess it, brought my heart into my mouth.

It was such a noise as a person would make scratching loudly with a finger-nail; it came from under the knapsack which served me for a pillow, and it was thrice repeated before I had time to sit up and turn about. Nothing was to be seen, nothing more was to be heard, but a few of these mysterious rustlings far and near, and the ceaseless accompaniment of the river and the frogs. I learned next day that the chestnut gardens are infested by rats; rustling, chirping, and scraping were probably all due to these; but the puzzle, for the moment, was insoluble, and I had to compose myself for sleep, as best I could, in wondering uncertainty about my neighbours.

I was wakened in the grey of the morning (Monday, 30th September) by the sound of foot-steps not far off upon the stones, and opening my eyes, I beheld a peasant going by among the chestnuts by a footpath that I had not hitherto observed. He turned his head neither to the right nor to the left, and disappeared in a few strides among the foliage. Here was an escape! But it was plainly more than time to be moving. The peasantry were abroad; scarce less terrible to me in my nondescript position than the soldiers of Captain Poul to an undaunted Camisard. I fed Modestine with what haste I could; but as I was returning to my sack, I saw a man and a boy come down the hillside in a direction crossing mine. They unintelligibly hailed me, and I replied with inarticulate but cheerful sounds, and hurried forward to get into my gaiters. The pair, who seemed to be father and son, came slowly up to the plateau, and stood close beside me for some time in silence. The bed was open, and I saw with regret my revolver lying patently disclosed on the blue wool. At last, after they had looked me all over, and the silence had grown laughably embarrassing, the man demanded in what seemed unfriendly tones:

'You have slept here?'

'Yes,' said I. 'As you see.'

'Why?' he asked.

'My faith,' I answered lightly, 'I was tired.'

He next inquired where I was going and what I had had for dinner; and then, without the least transition, 'C'est bien,' he added, 'come along.' And he and his son, without another word, turned off to the next chestnut-tree but one, which they set to pruning. The thing had passed of more simply than I hoped. He was a grave, respectable man; and his unfriendly voice did not imply that he thought he was speaking to a criminal, but merely to an inferior.

I was soon on the road, nibbling a cake of chocolate and seriously occupied with a case of conscience. Was I to pay for my night's lodging? I had slept ill, the bed was full of fleas in the shape of ants, there was no water in the room, the very dawn had neglected to call me in the morning. I might have

80

missed a train, had there been any in the neighbourhood to catch. Clearly, I was dissatisfied with my entertainment; and I decided I should not pay unless I met a beggar.

The valley looked even lovelier by morning; and soon the road descended to the level of the river. Here, in a place where many straight and prosperous chestnuts stood together, making an aisle upon a swarded terrace, I made my morning toilette in the water of the Tarn. It was marvellously clear, thrillingly cool; the soap-suds disappeared as if by magic in the swift current, and the white boulders gave one a model for cleanliness. To wash in one of God's rivers in the open air seems to me a sort of cheerful solemnity or semi-pagan act of worship. To dabble among dishes in a bedroom may perhaps make clean the body; but the imagination takes no share in such a cleansing. I went on with a light and peaceful heart, and sang psalms to the spiritual ear as I advanced.

Suddenly up came an old woman, who point-blank demanded alms.

'Good,' thought I; 'here comes the waiter with the bill.'

And I paid for my night's lodging on the spot. Take it how you please, but this was the first and the last beggar that I met with during all my tour. A step or two farther I was overtaken by an old man in a brown nightcap, clear-eyed, weather-beaten, with a faint excited smile.

A little girl followed him, driving two sheep and a goat; but she kept in our wake, while the old man walked beside me and talked about the morning and the valley.

It was not much past six; and for healthy people who have slept enough, that is an hour of expansion and of open and trustful talk.

'Connaissez-vous le Seigneur?' he said at length.

I asked him what Seigneur he meant; but he only repeated the question with more emphasis and a look in his eyes denoting hope and interest.

'Ah,' said I, pointing upwards, 'I understand you now. Yes, I know Him; He is the best of acquaintances.'

The old man said he was delighted. 'Hold,' he added, striking his bosom; 'it makes me happy here.' There were a few who knew the Lord in these valleys, he went on to tell me; not many, but a few. 'Many are called,' he quoted, 'and few chosen.'

'My father,' said I, 'it is not easy to say who know the Lord; and it is none of our business. Protestants and Catholics, and even those who worship stones, may know Him and be known by Him; for He has made all.'

I did not know I was so good a preacher.

The old man assured me he thought as I did, and repeated his expressions of pleasure at meeting me. 'We are so few,' he said. 'They call us Moravians here; but down in the Department of Gard, where there are also a good number, they are called Derbists, after an English pastor.'

I began to understand that I was figuring, in questionable taste, as a member of some sect to me unknown; but I was more pleased with the pleasure of my companion than embarrassed by my own equivocal position. Indeed, I can see no dishonesty in not avowing a difference; and especially in these high matters, where we have all a sufficient assurance that, whoever may be in the wrong, we ourselves are not completely in the right. The truth is much talked about; but this old man in a brown nightcap showed himself so simple, sweet, and friendly, that I am not unwilling to profess myself his convert. He was, as a matter of fact, a Plymouth Brother. Of what that involves in the way of doctrine I have no idea nor the time to inform myself; but I know right well that we are all embarked upon a troublesome world, the children of one Father, striving in many essential points to do and to become the same. And although it was somewhat in a mistake that he shook hands with me so often and showed himself so ready to receive my words, that was a mistake of the truth-finding sort. For charity begins blindfold; and only through a series of similar misapprehensions rises at length into a settled principle of love and patience, and a firm belief in all our fellow-men. If I deceived this good old man, in the like manner I would willingly go on to deceive others. And if ever at length, out of our separate and sad ways, we should all come together into one common house, I have a hope, to which I cling dearly, that my mountain Plymouth Brother will hasten to shake hands with me again.

Thus, talking like Christian and Faithful by the way, he and I came down upon a hamlet by the Tarn. It was but a humble place, called La Vernede, with less than a dozen houses, and a Protestant chapel on a knoll. Here he dwelt; and here, at the inn, I ordered my breakfast. The inn was kept by an agreeable young man, a stone-breaker on the road, and his sister, a pretty and engaging girl. The village schoolmaster dropped in to speak with the stranger. And these were all Protestants - a fact which pleased me more than I should have expected; and, what pleased me still more, they seemed all upright and simple people. The Plymouth Brother hung round me with a sort of yearning interest, and returned at least thrice to make sure I was enjoying my meal. His behaviour touched me deeply at the time, and even now moves me in recollection. He feared to intrude, but he would not willingly forego one moment of my society; and he seemed never weary of shaking me by the hand.

When all the rest had drifted off to their day's work, I sat for near half an hour with the young mistress of the house, who talked pleasantly over her seam of the chestnut harvest, and the beauties of the Tarn, and old family affections, broken up when young folk go from home, yet still subsisting. Hers, I am sure, was a sweet nature, with a country plainness and much delicacy underneath; and he who takes her to his heart will doubtless be a fortunate young man.

The valley below La Vernede pleased me more and more as I went forward. Now the hills approached from either hand, naked and crumbling, and walled in the river between cliffs; and now the valley widened and became green. The road led me past the old castle of Miral on a steep; past a battlemented monastery, long since broken up and turned into a church and parsonage; and past a cluster of black roofs, the village of Cocures, sitting among vineyards, and meadows, and orchards thick with red apples, and where, along the highway, they were knocking down walnuts from the roadside trees, and gathering them in sacks and baskets. The hills, however much the vale might open, were still tall and bare, with cliffy battlements and here and there a pointed summit; and the Tarn still rattled through the stones with a mountain noise. I had been led, by bagmen of a picturesque turn of mind, to expect a horrific country after the heart of Byron; but to my Scottish eyes it seemed smiling and plentiful, as the weather still gave an impression of high summer to my Scottish body; although the chestnuts were already picked out by the autumn, and the poplars, that here began to mingle with them, had turned into pale gold against the approach of winter.

There was something in this landscape, smiling although wild, that explained to me the spirit of the Southern Covenanters. Those who took to the hills for conscience' sake in Scotland had all gloomy and bedevilled thoughts; for once that they received God's comfort they would be twice engaged with Satan; but the Camisards had only bright and supporting visions. They dealt much more in blood, both given and taken; yet I find no obsession of the Evil One in their records. With a light conscience, they pursued their life in these rough times and circumstances. The soul of Seguier, let us not forget, was like a garden. They knew they were on God's side, with a knowledge that has no parallel among the Scots; for the Scots, although they might be certain of the cause, could never rest confident of the person.

'We flew,' says one old Camisard, 'when we heard the sound of psalm-singing, we flew as if with wings. We felt within us an animating ardour, a transporting desire. The feeling cannot be expressed in words. It is a thing that must have been experienced to be understood. However weary we might be, we thought no more of our weariness, and grew light so soon as the psalms fell upon our ears.'

The valley of the Tarn and the people whom I met at La Vernede not only explain to me this passage, but the twenty years of suffering which those, who were so stiff and so bloody when once they betook themselves to war, endured with the meekness of children and the constancy of saints and peasants.

Chapter Fourteen

Florac

O N A BRANCH of the Tarn stands Florac, the seat of a sub-prefecture, with an old castle, an alley of planes, many quaint street-corners, and a live fountain welling from the hill. It is notable, besides, for handsome women, and as one of the two capitals, Alais being the other, of the country of the Camisards.

The landlord of the inn took me, after I had eaten, to an adjoining cafe, where I, or rather my journey, became the topic of the afternoon. Every one had some suggestion for my guidance; and the sub-prefectorial map was fetched from the sub-prefecture itself, and much thumbed among coffee-cups and glasses of liqueur. Most of these kind advisers were Protestant, though I observed that Protestant and Catholic intermingled in a very easy manner; and it surprised me to see what a lively memory still subsisted of the religious war. Among the hills of the south-west, by Mauchline, Cumnock, or Carsphairn, in isolated farms or in the manse, serious Presbyterian people still recall the days of the great persecution, and the graves of local martyrs are still piously regarded.

But in towns and among the so-called better classes, I fear that these old doings have become an idle tale. If you met a mixed company in the King's Arms at Wigton, it is not likely that the talk would run on Covenanters. Nay, at Muirkirk of Glenluce, I found the beadle's wife had not so much as heard of Prophet Peden. But these Cevenols were proud of their ancestors in quite another sense.

Florac: "one of the two capitals of the country of the Camisards."

The war was their chosen topic; its exploits were their own patent of nobility; and where a man or a race has had but one adventure, and that heroic, we must expect and pardon some prolixity of reference. They told me the country was still full of legends hitherto uncollected; I heard from them about Cavalier's descendants - not direct descendants, be it understood, but only cousins or nephews - who were still prosperous people in the scene of the boy-general's exploits; and one farmer had seen the bones of old combatants dug up into the air of an afternoon in the nineteenth century, in a field where the ancestors had fought, and the great-grandchildren were peaceably ditching.

Later in the day one of the Protestant pastors was so good as to visit me: a young man, intelligent and polite, with whom I passed an hour or two in talk. Florac, he told me, is part Protestant, part Catholic; and the difference in religion is usually doubled by a difference in politics. You may judge of my surprise, coming as I did from such a babbling purgatorial Poland of a place as Monastier, when I learned that the population lived together on very quiet terms; and there was even an exchange of hospitalities between households thus doubly separated. Black Camisard and White Camisard, militiaman and Miquelet and dragoon, Protestant prophet and Catholic cadet of the White Cross, they had all been sabring and shooting, burning, pillaging, and murdering, their hearts hot with indignant passion; and here, after a hundred and seventy years, Protestant is still Protestant, Catholic still Catholic, in mutual toleration and mild amity of life. But the race of man, like that indomitable nature whence it sprang, has medicating virtues of its own; the years and seasons bring various harvests; the sun returns after the rain; and mankind outlives secular animosities, as a single man awakens from the passions of a day. We judge our ancestors from a more divine position; and the dust being a little laid with several centuries, we can see both sides adorned with human virtues and fighting with a show of right.

I have never thought it easy to be just, and find it daily even harder than I thought. I own I met these Protestants with a delight and a sense of coming home. I was accustomed to speak their language, in another and deeper sense of the word than that which distinguishes between French and English; for the true Babel is a divergence upon morals. And hence I could hold more free communication with the Protestants, and judge them more justly, than the Catholics. Father Apollinaris may pair off with my mountain Plymouth Brother as two guileless and devout old men; yet I ask myself if I had as ready a feeling for the virtues of the Trappist; or, had I been a Catholic, if I should have felt so warmly to the dissenter of La

Vernede. With the first I was on terms of mere forbearance; but with the other, although only on a misunderstanding and by keeping on selected points, it was still possible to hold converse and exchange some honest thoughts. In this world of imperfection we gladly welcome even partial intimacies. And if we find but one to whom we can speak out of our heart freely, with whom we can walk in love and simplicity without dissimulation, we have no ground of quarrel with the world or God.

Chapter Fifteen

In the Valley of the Mimente

O N TUESDAY, 1st October, we left Florac late in the afternoon, a tired donkey and tired donkey-driver. A little way up the Tarnon, a covered bridge of wood introduced us into the valley of the Mimente. Steep rocky red mountains overhung the stream; great oaks and chestnuts grew upon the slopes or in stony terraces; here and there was a red field of millet or a few apple-trees studded with red apples; and the road passed hard by two black hamlets, one with an old castle atop to please the heart of the tourist.

It was difficult here again to find a spot fit for my encampment. Even under the oaks and chestnuts the ground had not only a very rapid slope, but was heaped with loose stones; and where there was no timber the hills descended to the stream in a red precipice tufted with heather. The sun had left the highest peak in front of me, and the valley was full of the lowing sound of herdsmen's horns as they recalled the flocks into the stable, when I spied a bight of meadow some way below the roadway in an angle of the river. Thither I descended, and, tying Modestine provisionally to a tree, proceeded to investigate the neighbourhood. A grey pearly evening shadow filled the glen; objects at a little distance grew indistinct and melted bafflingly into each other; and the darkness was rising steadily like an exhalation. I approached a great oak which grew in the meadow, hard by the river's brink; when to my disgust the voices of children fell upon my ear, and I beheld a house round the angle on the other bank. I had half a mind to pack and be gone again, but the growing darkness moved me to remain. I had only to make no noise until the night was fairly come, and trust to the dawn to call me early in the morning. But it was hard to be annoyed by neighbours in such a great hotel.

A hollow underneath the oak was my bed. Before I had fed Modestine and arranged my sack, three stars were already brightly shining, and the others were beginning dimly to appear. I slipped down to the river, which looked very black among its rocks, to fill my can; and dined with a good appetite in the dark, for I scrupled to light a lantern while so near a house. The moon, which I had seen a pallid crescent all afternoon, faintly illuminated the summit of the hills, but not a ray fell into the bottom of the glen where I was lying. The oak rose before me like a pillar of darkness; and overhead the heartsome stars were set in the face of the night.

No one knows the stars who has not slept, as the French happily put it, a la belle etoile. He may know all their names and distances and magnitudes, and yet be ignorant of what alone concerns mankind, - their serene and gladsome influence on the mind. The greater part of poetry is about the stars; and very justly, for they are themselves the most classical of poets. These same far-away worlds, sprinkled like tapers or shaken together like a diamond dust upon the sky, had looked not otherwise to Roland or Cavalier, when, in the words of the latter, they had 'no other tent but the sky, and no other bed than my mother earth.'

All night a strong wind blew up the valley, and the acorns fell pattering over me from the oak. Yet, on this first night of October, the air was as mild as May, and I slept with the fur thrown back.

I was much disturbed by the barking of a dog, an animal that I fear more than any wolf. A dog is vastly braver, and is besides supported by the sense of duty. If you kill a wolf, you meet with encouragement and praise; but if you kill a dog, the sacred rights of property and the domestic affections come clamouring round you for redress. At the end of a fagging day, the sharp cruel note of a dog's bark is in itself a keen annoyance; and to a tramp like myself, he represents the sedentary and respectable world in its most hostile form. There is something of the clergyman or the lawyer about this engaging animal; and if he were not amenable to stones, the boldest man would shrink from travelling afoot. I respect dogs much in the domestic circle; but on the highway, or sleeping afield, I both detest and fear them.

90

I was wakened next morning (Wednesday, October 2nd) by the same dog—for I knew his bark - making a charge down the bank, and then, seeing me sit up, retreating again with great alacrity. The stars were not yet quite extinguished. The heaven was of that enchanting mild grey-blue of the early morn. A still clear light began to fall, and the trees on the hillside were outlined sharply against the sky. The wind had veered more to the north, and no longer reached me in the glen; but as I was going on with my preparations, it drove a white cloud very swiftly over the hill-top; and looking up, I was surprised to see the cloud dyed with gold. In these high regions of the air, the sun was already shining as at noon. If only the clouds travelled high enough, we should see the same thing all night long. For it is always daylight in the fields of space.

As I began to go up the valley, a draught of wind came down it out of the seat of the sunrise, although the clouds continued to run overhead in an almost contrary direction. A few steps farther, and I saw a whole hillside gilded with the sun; and still a little beyond, between two peaks, a centre of dazzling brilliancy appeared floating in the sky, and I was once more face to face with the big bonfire that occupies the kernel of our system.

I met but one human being that forenoon, a dark military-looking wayfarer, who carried a game-bag on a baldric; but he made a remark that seems worthy of record. For when I asked him if he were Protestant or Catholic - 'Oh,' said he, 'I make no shame of my religion. I am a Catholic.'

He made no shame of it! The phrase is a piece of natural statistics; for it is the language of one in a minority. I thought with a smile of Bavile and his dragoons, and how you may ride rough-shod over a religion for a century, and leave it only the more lively for the friction. Ireland is still Catholic; the Cevennes still Protestant. It is not a basketful of law-papers, nor the hoofs and pistol-butts of a regiment of horse, that can change one tittle of a ploughman's thoughts. Outdoor rustic people have not many ideas, but such as they have are hardy plants, and thrive flourishingly in persecution. One who has grown a long while in the sweat of laborious noons, and under the stars at night, a frequenter of hills and forests, an old honest countryman, has, in the end, a sense of communion with the powers of the universe, and amicable relations towards his God. Like my mountain Plymouth Brother, he knows the Lord. His religion does not repose upon a choice of logic; it is the poetry of the man's experience, the philosophy of the history of his life. God, like a great power, like a great shining sun, has appeared to this simple fellow in the course of years, and become the ground and essence of his least reflections; and you may change creeds and dogmas by authority, or proclaim a new religion with the sound of trumpets, if you will; but here is a man who has his own thoughts, and will stubbornly adhere to them in good and evil. He is a Catholic, a Protestant, or a Plymouth Brother, in the same indefeasible sense that a man is not a woman, or a woman not a man. For he could not vary from his faith, unless he could eradicate all memory of the past, and, in a strict and not a conventional meaning, change his mind.

Chapter Sixteen

The heart of the country

I WAS NOW DRAWING near to Cassagnas, a cluster of black roofs upon the hillside, in this wild valley, among chestnut gardens, and looked upon in the clear air by many rocky peaks. The road along the Mimente is yet new, nor have the mountaineers recovered their surprise when the first cart arrived at Cassagnas. But although it lay thus apart from the current of men's business, this hamlet had already made a figure in the history of France. Hard by, in caverns of the mountain, was one of the five arsenals of the Camisards; where they laid up clothes and corn and arms against necessity, forged bayonets and sabres, and made themselves gunpowder with willow charcoal and saltpetre boiled in kettles. To the same caves, amid this multifarious industry, the sick and wounded were brought up to heal; and there they were visited by the two surgeons, Chabrier and Tavan, and secretly nursed by women of the neighbourhood.

Of the five legions into which the Camisards were divided, it was the oldest and the most obscure that had its magazines by Cassagnas. This was the band of Spirit Seguier; men who had joined their voices with his in the 68th Psalm as they marched down by night on the archpriest of the Cevennes. Seguier, promoted to heaven, was succeeded by Salomon Couderc, whom Cavalier treats in his memoirs as chaplain-general to the whole army of the Camisards. He was a prophet; a great reader of the heart, who admitted people to the sacrament or refused them, by 'intensively viewing every man' between the eyes; and had the most of the Scriptures off by rote. And this was surely happy; since in a surprise in August 1703, he lost his mule, his portfolios, and his Bible.

It is only strange that they were not surprised more often and more effectually; for this legion of Cassagnas was truly patriarchal in its theory of war, and camped without sentries, leaving that duty to the angels of the God for whom they fought. This is a token, not only of their faith, but of the trackless country where they harboured. M. de Caladon, taking a stroll one fine day, walked without warning into their midst, as he might have walked into 'a flock of sheep in a plain,' and found some asleep and some awake and psalm-singing. A traitor had need of no recommendation to insinuate himself among their ranks, beyond 'his faculty of singing psalms'; and even the prophet Salomon 'took him into a particular friendship.' Thus, among their intricate hills, the rustic troop subsisted; and history can attribute few exploits to them but sacraments and ecstasies.

People of this tough and simple stock will not, as I have just been saying, prove variable in religion; nor will they get nearer to apostasy than a mere external conformity like that of Naaman in the house of Rimmon. When Louis XVI., in the words of the edict, 'convinced by the uselessness of a century of persecutions, and rather from necessity than sympathy,' granted at last a royal grace of toleration, Cassagnas was still Protestant; and to a man, it is so to this day. There is, indeed, one family that is not Protestant, but neither is it Catholic. It is that of a Catholic cure in revolt, who has taken to his bosom a schoolmistress. And his conduct, it is worth noting, is disapproved by the Protestant villagers.

'It is a bad idea for a man,' said one, 'to go back from his engagements.'

The villagers whom I saw seemed intelligent after a countrified fashion, and were all plain and dignified in manner. As a Protestant myself, I was well looked upon, and my acquaintance with history gained me further respect. For we had something not unlike a religious controversy at table, a gendarme and a merchant with whom I dined being both strangers to the place, and Catholics. The young men of the house stood round and supported me; and the whole discussion was tolerantly conducted, and surprised a man brought up among the infinitesimal and contentious differences of Scotland. The merchant, indeed, grew a little warm, and was far less pleased than some others with my historical acquirements. But the gendarme was mighty easy over it all.

'It's a bad idea for a man to change,' said he; and the remark was generally applauded. That was not the opinion of the priest and soldier at Our Lady of theSnows. But this is a different race; and perhaps the same great-heartedness that upheld them to resist, now enables them to differ in a kind spirit. For courage respects courage; but where a faith has been trodden out, we may look for a mean and narrow population. The true work of Bruce and Wallace was the union of the nations; not that they should stand apart a while longer, skirmishing upon their borders; but that, when the time came, they might unite with self-respect.

The merchant was much interested in my journey, and thought it dangerous to sleep afield.

'There are the wolves,' said he; 'and then it is known you are an Englishman. The English have always long purses, and it might very well enter into some one's head to deal you an ill blow some night.'

I told him I was not much afraid of such accidents; and at any rate judged it unwise to dwell upon alarms or consider small perils in the arrangement of life. Life itself, I submitted, was a far too risky business as a whole to make each additional particular of danger worth regard. 'Something,' said I, 'might burst in your inside any day of the week, and there would be an end of you, if you were locked into your room with three turns of the key.'

'Cependant,' said he, 'coucher dehors!'

'God,' said I, 'is everywhere.'

'Cependant, coucher dehors!' he repeated, and his voice was eloquent of terror.

He was the only person, in all my voyage, who saw anything hardy in so simple a proceeding; although many considered it superfluous. Only one, on the other hand, professed much delight in the idea; and that was my Plymouth Brother, who cried out, when I told him I sometimes preferred sleeping under the stars to a close and noisy ale-house, 'Now I see that you know the Lord!'

The merchant asked me for one of my cards as I was leaving, for he said I should be something to talk of in the future, and desired me to make a note of his request and reason; a desire with which I have thus complied.

A little after two I struck across the Mimente, and took a rugged path southward up a hillside covered with loose stones and tufts of heather. At the top, as is the habit of the country, the path disappeared; and I left my she-ass munching heather, and went forward alone to seek a road.

I was now on the separation of two vast water-sheds; behind me all the streams were bound for the Garonne and the Western Ocean; before me was the basin of the Rhone. Hence, as from the Lozere, you can see in clear weather the shining of the Gulf of Lyons; and perhaps from here the soldiers of Salomon may have watched for the topsails of Sir Cloudesley Shovel, and the long-promised aid from England. You may take this ridge as lying in the heart of the country of the Camisards; four of the five legions camped all round it and almost within view - Salomon and Joani to the north, Castanet and Roland to the south; and when Julien had finished his famous work, the devastation of the High Cevennes, which lasted all through October and November 1703, and during which four hundred and sixty villages and hamlets were, with fire and pickaxe, utterly subverted, a man standing on this eminence would have looked forth upon a silent, smokeless, and dispeopled land. Time and man's activity have now repaired these ruins; Cassagnas is once more roofed and sending up domestic smoke; and in the chestnut gardens, in low and leafy corners, many a prosperous farmer returns, when the day's work is done, to his children and bright hearth. And still it was perhaps the wildest view of all my journey. Peak upon peak, chain upon chain of hills ran surging southward, channelled and sculptured by the winter streams, feathered from head to foot with chestnuts, and here and there breaking out into a coronal of cliffs. The sun, which was still far from setting, sent a drift of misty gold across the hill-tops, but the valleys were already plunged in a profound and quiet shadow.

A very old shepherd, hobbling on a pair of sticks, and wearing a black cap of liberty, as if in honour of his nearness to the grave, directed me to the road for St. Germain de Calberte. There was something solemn in the isolation of this infirm and ancient creature. Where he dwelt, how he got upon this high ridge, or how he proposed to get down again, were more than I could fancy. Not far off upon my right was the famous Plan de Font Morte, where Poul with his Armenian sabre slashed down the Camisards of Seguier. This, methought, might be some Rip van Winkle of the war, who had lost his comrades, fleeing before Poul, and wandered ever since upon the mountains. It might be news to him that Cavalier had surrendered, or Roland had fallen fighting with his back against an olive. And while I was thus working on my fancy, I heard him hailing in broken tones, and saw him waving me to come back with one of his two sticks. I had already got some way past him; but, leaving Modestine once more, retraced my steps.

Alas, it was a very commonplace affair. The old gentleman had forgot to ask the pedlar what he sold, and wished to remedy this neglect.

I told him sternly, 'Nothing.'

'Nothing?' cried he.

I repeated 'Nothing,' and made off.

It's odd to think of, but perhaps I thus became as inexplicable to the old man as he had been to me.

The road lay under chestnuts, and though I saw a hamlet or two below me in the vale, and many lone houses of the chestnut farmers, it was a very solitary march all afternoon; and the evening began early underneath the trees. But I heard the voice of a woman singing some sad, old, endless ballad not far off. It seemed to be about love and a bel amoureux, her handsome sweetheart; and I wished I could have taken up the strain and answered her, as I went on upon my invisible woodland way, weaving, like Pippa in the poem, my own thoughts with hers. What could I have told her? Little enough; and yet all the heart requires. How the world gives and takes away, and brings sweethearts near only to separate them again into distant and strange lands; but to love is the great amulet which makes the world a garden; and 'hope, which comes to all,' outwears the accidents of life, and reaches with tremulous hand beyond the grave and death. Easy to say: yea, but also, by God's mercy, both easy and grateful to believe!

We struck at last into a wide white high-road carpeted with noiseless dust. The night had come; the moon had been shining for a long while upon the opposite mountain; when on turning a corner my donkey and I issued ourselves into her light. I had emptied out my brandy at Florac, for I could bear the stuff no longer, and replaced it with some generous and scented Volnay; and now I drank to the moon's sacred majesty upon the road. It was but a couple of mouthfuls; yet I became thenceforth unconscious of my limbs, and my blood flowed with luxury. Even Modestine was inspired by this purified nocturnal sunshine, and bestirred her little hoofs as to a livelier measure. The road wound and descended swiftly among masses of chestnuts. Hot dust rose from our feet and flowed away. Our two shadows - mine deformed with the knapsack, hers comically bestridden by the pack

- now lay before us clearly outlined on the road, and now, as we turned a corner, went off into the ghostly distance, and sailed along the mountain like clouds. From time to time a warm wind rustled down the valley, and set all the chestnuts dangling their bunches of foliage and fruit; the ear was filled with whispering music, and the shadows danced in tune. And next moment the breeze had gone by, and in all the valley nothing moved except our travelling feet. On the opposite slope, the monstrous ribs and gullies of the mountain were faintly designed in the moonshine; and high overhead, in some lone house, there burned one lighted window, one square spark of red in the huge field of sad nocturnal colouring.

At a certain point, as I went downward, turning many acute angles, the moon disappeared behind the hill; and I pursued my way in great darkness, until another turning shot me without preparation into St. Germain de Calberte. The place was asleep and silent, and buried in opaque night. Only from a single open door, some lamplight escaped upon the road to show me that I was come among men's habitations. The two last gossips of the evening, still talking by a garden wall, directed me to the inn. The landlady was getting her chicks to bed; the fire was already out, and had, not without grumbling, to be rekindled; half an hour later, and I must have gone supperless to roost.

Chapter Seventeen

The last day

WHEN I AWOKE (Thursday, 2nd October), and, hearing a great flourishing of cocks and chuckling of contented hens, betook me to the window of the clean and comfortable room where I had slept the night, I looked forth on a sunshiny morning in a deep vale of chestnut gardens. It was still early, and the cockcrows, and the slanting lights, and the long shadows encouraged me to be out and look round me.

St. Germain de Calberte is a great parish nine leagues round about. At the period of the wars, and immediately before the devastation, it was inhabited by two hundred and seventy-five families, of which only nine were Catholic; and it took the cure seventeen September days to go from house to house on horseback for a census. But the place itself, although capital of a canton, is scarce larger than a hamlet. It lies terraced across a steep slope in the midst of mighty chestnuts.

The Protestant chapel stands below upon a shoulder; in the midst of the town is the quaint old Catholic church. It was here that poor Du Chayla, the Christian martyr, kept his library and held a court of missionaries; here he had built his tomb, thinking to lie among a grateful population whom he had redeemed from error; and hither on the morrow of his death they brought the body, pierced with two-and-fifty wounds, to be interred. Clad in his priestly robes, he was laid out in state in the church. The cure, taking his text from Second Samuel, twentieth chapter and twelfth verse, 'And Amasa wallowed in his blood in the highway,' preached a rousing sermon, and exhorted his brethren to die each at his post, like their unhappy and illustrious superior. In the midst of this eloquence there came a breeze that Spirit Seguier was near at hand; and behold! all the assembly took to their horses' heels, some east, some west, and the cure himself as far as Alais.

Strange was the position of this little Catholic metropolis, a thimbleful of Rome, in such a wild and contrary neighbourhood. On the one hand, the legion of Salomon overlooked it from Cassagnas; on the other, it was cut off from assistance by the legion of Roland at Mialet. The cure, Louvrelenil, although he took a panic at the arch-priest's funeral, and so hurriedly decamped to Alais, stood well by his isolated pulpit, and thence uttered fulminations against the crimes of the Protestants. Salomon besieged the village for an hour and a half, but was beaten back. The militiamen, on guard before the cure's door, could be heard, in the black hours, singing Protestant psalms and holding friendly talk with the insurgents. And in the morning, although not a shot had been fired, there would not be a round of powder in their flasks. Where was it gone? All handed over to the Camisards for a consideration. Untrusty guardians for an isolated priest!

That these continual stirs were once busy in St. Germain de Calberte, the imagination with difficulty receives; all is now so quiet, the pulse of human life now beats so low and still in this hamlet of the mountains.Boys followed me a great way off, like a timid sort of lion-hunters; and people turned round to have a second look, or came out of their houses, as I went by. My passage was the first event, you would have fancied, since the Camisards. There was nothing rude or forward in this observation; it was but a pleased and wondering scrutiny, like that of oxen or the human infant; yet it wearied my spirits, and soon drove me from the street.

I took refuge on the terraces, which are here greenly carpeted with sward, and tried to imitate with a pencil the inimitable attitudes of the chestnuts as they bear up their canopy of leaves. Ever and again a little wind went by, and the nuts dropped all around me, with a light and dull sound, upon the sward. The noise was as of a thin fall of great hailstones; but there went with it a cheerful human sentiment of an approaching harvest and farmers rejoicing in their gains.

Looking up, I could see the brown nut peering through the husk, which was already gaping; and between the stems the eye embraced an amphitheatre of hill, sunlit and green with leaves.

I have not often enjoyed a place more deeply. I moved in an atmosphere of pleasure, and felt light and quiet and content. But perhaps it was not the place alone that so disposed my spirit. Perhaps some one was thinking of me in another country; or perhaps some thought of my own had come and gone unnoticed, and yet done me good. For some thoughts, which sure would be the most beautiful, vanish before we can rightly scan their features; as though a god, travelling by our green highways, should but open the door, give one smiling look into the house, and go again for ever.

Was it Apollo, or Mercury, or Love with folded wings? Who shall say? But we go the lighter about our business, and feel peace and pleasure in our hearts.

I dined with a pair of Catholics. They agreed in the condemnation of a young man, a Catholic, who had married a Protestant girl and gone over to the religion of his wife. A Protestant born they could understand and respect; indeed, they seemed to be of the mind of an old Catholic woman, who told me that same day there was no difference between the two sects, save that 'wrong was more wrong for the Catholic,' who had more light and guidance; but this of a man's desertion filled them with contempt.

'It is a bad idea for a man to change,' said one.

It may have been accidental, but you see how this phrase pursued me; and for myself, I believe it is the current philosophy in these parts. I have some difficulty in imagining a better. It's not only a great flight of confidence for a man to change his creed and go out of his family for heaven's sake; but the odds are - nay, and the hope is - that, with all this great transition in the eyes of man, he has not changed himself a airbreadth to the eyes of God. Honour to those who do so, for the wrench is sore. But it argues something narrow, whether of strength or weakness, whether of the prophet or the fool, in those who can take a sufficient interest in such infinitesimal and human operations, or who can quit a friendship for a doubtful process of the mind. And I think I should not leave my old creed for another, changing only words for other words; but by some brave reading, embrace it in spirit and truth, and find wrong as wrong for me as for the best of other communions.

The phylloxera was in the neighbourhood; and instead of wine we drank at dinner a more economical juice of the grape - La Parisienne, they call it. It is made by putting the fruit whole into a cask with water; one by one the berries ferment and burst; what is drunk during the day is supplied at night in water: so, with ever another pitcher from the well, and ever another grape exploding and giving out its strength, one cask of Parisienne may last a family till spring. It is, as the reader will anticipate, a feeble beverage, but very pleasant to the taste. What with dinner and coffee, it was long past three before I left St.Germain de Calberte. I went down beside the Gardon of Mialet, a great glaring watercourse devoid of water, and through St. Etienne de Vallee Francaise, or Val Francesque, as they used to call it; and towards evening began to ascend the hill of St. Pierre. It was a long and steep ascent. Behind me an empty carriage returning to St. Jean du Gard kept hard upon my tracks, and near the summit overtook me. The driver, like the rest of the world, was sure I was a pedlar; but, unlike others, he was sure of what I had to sell. He had noticed the blue wool which hung out of my pack at either end; and from this he had decided, beyond my power to alter his decision, that I dealt in blue-wool collars, such as decorate the neck of the French draught-horse.

I had hurried to the topmost powers of Modestine, for I dearly desired to see the view upon the other side before the day had faded. But it was night when I reached the summit; the moon was riding high and clear; and only a few grey streaks of twilight lingered in the west. A yawning valley, gulfed in blackness, lay like a hole in created nature at my feet; but the outline of the hills was sharp against the sky.

There was Mount Aigoal, the stronghold of Castanet. And Castanet, not only as an active undertaking leader, deserves some mention among Camisards; for there is a spray of rose among his laurel; and he showed how, even in a public tragedy, love will have its way. In the high tide of war he married, in his mountain citadel, a young and pretty lass called Mariette. There were great rejoicings; and the bridegroom released five-and-twenty prisoners in honour of the glad event. Seven months afterwards, Mariette, the Princess of the Cevennes, as they called her in derision, fell into the hands of the authorities, where it was like to have gone hard with her. But Castanet was a man of execution, and loved his wife. He fell on Valleraugue, and got a lady there for a hostage; and for the first and last time in that war there was an exchange of prisoners. Their daughter, pledge of some starry night upon Mount Aigoal, has left descendants to this day.

Modestine and I - it was our last meal together - had a snack upon the top of St. Pierre, I on a heap of stones, she standing by me in the moonlight and decorously eating bread out of my hand.

The poor brute would eat more heartily in this manner; for she had a sort of affection for me, which I was soon to betray.

It was a long descent upon St. Jean du Gard, and we met no one but a carter, visible afar off by the glint of the moon on his extinguished lantern. Before ten o'clock we had got in and were at supper; fifteen miles and a stiff hill in little beyond six hours!

The château at St-Jean du Gard

Chapter Eighteen

Farewell, Modestine!

O N EXAMINATION, on the morning of October 3rd, Modestine was pronounced unfit for travel. She would need at least two days' repose, according to the ostler; but I was now eager to reach Alais for my letters; and, being in a civilised country of stage-coaches, I determined to sell my lady friend and be off by the diligence that afternoon. Our yesterday's march, with the testimony of the driver who had pursued us up the long hill of St. Pierre, spread a favourable notion of my donkey's capabilities. Intending purchasers were aware of an unrivalled opportunity. Before ten I had an offer of twenty-five francs; and before noon, after a desperate engagement, I sold her, saddle and all, for five-and-thirty. The pecuniary gain is not obvious, but I had bought freedom into the bargain.

St Jean du Gard is a large place, and largely Protestant. The maire, a Protestant, asked me to help him in a small matter which is itself characteristic of the country. The young women of the Cevennes profit by the common religion and the difference of the language to go largely as governesses into England; and here was one, a native of Mialet, struggling with English circulars from two different agencies in London. I gave what help I could; and volunteered some advice, which struck me as being excellent.

One thing more I note. The phylloxera has ravaged the vineyards in this neighbourhood; and in the early morning, under some chestnuts by the river, I found a party of men working with a cider-press. I could not at first make out what they were after, and asked one fellow to explain.

'Making cider,' he said. 'Oui, c'est comme ca. Comme dans le nord!'

There was a ring of sarcasm in his voice: the country was going to the devil.

It was not until I was fairly seated by the driver, and rattling through a rocky valley with dwarf olives, that I became aware of my bereavement. I had lost Modestine. Up to that moment I had thought I hated her; but now she was gone,

'And oh! The difference to me!'

For twelve days we had been fast companions; we had travelled upwards of a hundred and twenty miles, crossed several respectable ridges, and jogged along with our six legs by many a rocky and many a boggy by-road. After the first day, although sometimes I was hurt and distant in manner, I still kept my patience; and as for her, poor soul! she had come to regard me as a god. She loved to eat out of my hand. She was patient, elegant in form, the colour of an ideal mouse, and inimitably small. Her faults were those of her race and sex; her virtues were her own. Farewell, and if for ever - Father Adam wept when he sold her to me; after I had sold her in my turn, I was tempted to follow his example; and being alone with a stage-driver and four or five agreeable young men, I did not hesitate to yield to my emotion.

In the Footsteps of RLS ...

... and the Paths of Modestine

Useful information for modern travellers on the Stevenson Trail and beyond

by

Laurence Phillips

IT WAS ON THE VERY CUSP OF MIDSUMMER, in the middle of the week, halfway along the Gorges of the Tarn and two months short of my early middle age, that finally I understood the concept of the Sabbath.

Every Friday night until I was 21, and a good many more since then, I have watched my mother greet the twilight with the lighting of candles and my father begin reciting "It was evening and it was morning, the seventh day". However, it was not until overwhelmed by the grandeur, glory and mortal impossibility of Creation that I appreciated the need, even for Divinity, to stand back from the week's work and take stock. On the seventh day, He rested.

Sitting back in the boat, trailing my fingers in the fast flowing water, lifting my eyes up unto the hills and gasping at the sheer majesty of it all, I marvelled. And I understood. It was good.

It was good, more than a century before my own private epiphany, for Robert Louis Stevenson, who stood on the threshold of the Lozère, looked across the mountains to the distant Mediterranean and, as he declared, "a view into the hazy air of heaven".

It is almost impossible to believe that Lozère is in France. It seems just too big to have been kept secret for so long, so close to those cities and regions we all know so well. By rights one should travel for days or weeks to find the place, a 90-minute flight from London and a couple of hours on the road seems too easy. But, marked out by the Cevennes, the granite scored Margaride and those Tarn Gorges, this territory has left its footprint on history and literature, neither subdued nor compromised by tourism. There is a city in there somewhere, but it is Mende, and not on the cosmopolitan party circuit. The area, north of Montpellier and south of the Auvergne volcanos, is known for the land itself rather than man's 'civilising' imprint. I was told that there were four traffic lights in Lozère, but we drove for days and never found one. And no Big Mac had been known to take the place of a rustic sandwich within its boundaries until the 21st century was well within its stride.

Stevenson passed through on his famous *Travels With A Donkey* – a tale much loved in France and probably outselling *Treasure Island* in these parts. Today's visitors may rent donkeys to carry their kit on a hiking trail in Stevenson's footprints, overnighting on farms and in chambres d'hôtes.

On my first midsummer visit to this bypassed paradise, we, pressed for time, opted for an air-conditioned car to eat up the miles – its refreshing chill against an outside temperature nudging towards the 40-mark leading it to be dubbed the Frigomobile. On later trips, just passing through the area en route from Paris or London to the Med, I have sneaked onto the old path in order to spend a weekend or even just an afternoon in Modestine country and over to other unadulterated corners of the Lozère.

Like a reluctant Stevenson and an ardent Titania, I too am enamoured of an ass, and so could not pass through this land without meeting a donkey or two. On my inaugural odyssey, we stopped, before joining the RLS trail for lunch at the Domaine des Boissets, a tiny hamlet on the Causse de Sauveterre, which freezes in time the rustic architecture of the area. The farm donkeys will chew your most treasured possessions and roll their eyes at you in a most satisfactory manner. Wander through barns to enjoy exhibitions of farming and village life. Jerome, one of the youngsters managing the farm, rustled up a fabulous lunch to his grandmother's recipes. Several summers on, I still salivate at the memory of amazing aubergine and barnyard fare!

If donkeys are not enough, stay north. The werewolf legend of the Bête de Gevaudan, a thrilling tale of wild landscapes littered with virginal corpses, is as gothic as they come, and provided lip-smackingly good copy for RLS as he told himself horror stories at bedtime during his nights under a southern sky. We may no longer encounter the creature Stevenson dubbed a lupine Napoleon Bonaparte, Nonetheless, aficionados visit the sanctuary at Gevaudan, sanctioned by Brigitte Bardot, where wolfpacks still roam.

Rely neither on beasts nor myths for bloodthirsty yarns. The untamed topography provided the backdrop for the Camisard revolt of 1702. When Protestantism was outlawed, Huguenots practiced their religion in secret, holding services in cellars or preaching high on the hillside, with an eye alert for raids from the authorities. Camisards won their name from their camises, or chemises, white shirts worn at night for easy recognition. At the Musée du Désert (just across the county border in Mialet), glimpse the clandestine world of the closet protestant, and at the delightful village of Le Pont de Montvert (at the heart of the Stevenson trail, and where RLS recounts the story) see where rebellion became bloody, and the hunted turned on their tormentors.

If Le Pont de Montvert is an essential halt, then so must the lover of the truly picturesque deflect his compass from the literary pilgrims' route to find pleasures bypassed by Stevenson and Modestine, and detour towards St Enemie, capital of quaint, and as good a point as any to make one's way down to La Malène and board a boat, to be punted by garrulous bataliers along the fast flowing waters of the Tarn Gorges. The unwritten story of the waters that cleave their way through the cliffs is evocative stuff: An old stone house perched on high may be where the young Jacqueline Bouvier spent a summer long before she ever dreamt of the surnames Kennedy or Onnasis; the rock may rise 50 metres or 500 metres above your head as you lie back, your fingers teasing the sheet of pure water that divides the carp from the dragonfly. The facts dance through your mind with as little purpose as truant boys diving and splashing from rocks on the wrong side of the river. As a travel writer, I should have made notes; have retained the dates and names that make up the history of this place. But here, eyes towards an impeccably framed heaven, garlanded with trees, rocks and sunny-day rainbows, is where I learnt the very meaning of the Sabbath, and the value of rest.

Nights in Lozère are as special as the days. If the demands of the modern traveller keep us from spending the hours of darkness gazing at stars framed by pine trees from the place beneath, then chambres d'hôte provide a warm welcome:

Those, on the donkey trail, may yet tether their own daughters of Modestine and overnight at the Maison Victoire in Finiels, just beyond Pont de Montvert, where, at dusk, guests play guitars and sing a song at twilight. Or at the Refuge du Maure in Cheylard, where a chef who has prepared feasts for statesmen, considers supper for weary ramblers. I have dined in Logis de France comfort at La Lozerette at Cocorès and passed a tureen around the modest dining room at the Hotel la Source at Chasseradès.

I have strayed from the Stevenson path and discovered other welcomes along other byways; supping with fellow travellers under the walnut tree of the Maison de Marius at Quézac, eating, drinking and talking 'til well past bedtime, and on the morrow breakfasting on home-made pear and ginger jams in the garden. And I have indulged my sense of grandeur in the magnificent listed palatial setting of the Château de la Caze at La Malène on the Tarn, where gastronomy comes as standard, the view is more than anyone of us deserves, and where silently I toasted the sunset and moonrise of my first true Sabbath.

110

The Stevenson Trail today

THE JOURNEY IS PUNCTUATED with wild berries and scrumping opportunities, carpeted with a Russian roulette tapis of delicious mushrooms and deadly toadstools and canopied with slender blinked-lashes of fine filtered sunlight through dappled vaults of not-yet-autumn leaves. Lanes and byways, forgotten railway lines, wide-open fields on improbably high plateaux, curving mountain roads gaping down into valleys and vistas untouched by time. From the undulating volcanos of Auvergne to the deep woody secrets of the Cevennes, this is Stevenson Country.

Robert Louis Stevenson's original route is but randomly sketched in the travelogue. He himself took so many wrong turns, missed several easy goals and trotted down enough unconsidered paths to give us an impression, rather than a faithful record of the trail. Tarmac has since come to some of the roads he may have taken, so a modern traveller using a map and literary references might be lured onto a laborious traffic-dodging hike. Happily in 1993 the French rambling association (France has official authorities for almost every aspect of life) created the hikers trail GR70, which, with daubs of red and white paint on tree trunks and posts, follows the Stevensonian ideal cross stiles, miles and trials, capturing the essence and spirit of the original journey, and where one may pass many days

without seeing any anachronistic improvement tracing the centuries that followed that first adventure of 1878.

The modern RLS may walk alone or with friends, may take the dog along without the harsh effects of too many days of rough roads on tender paws.

Guided by daubs of red and white paint

The pilgrim may call upon a tour operator to carry luggage from point to point, hitch-up a rucksack and sleeping bag or even, as did our hero, employ a donkey to bear the burden. The hardy may risk a bicycle; the cautious select some choice slice of the route for walking, then retire on four wheels to a cosy inn or trout stream.

The first stretch of the trail takes in the Velay of the Southern Auvergne, cupped by calm and long-spent volcanos; roughness of a forgotten past soothed and smoothed into a kinder country by gentle greenery, watered by the serpentine meanderings of the river Loire and tinged with the verdant palette of fields of lentils and forests of pine.

Between the Lac du Bouchet, that Stevenson missed, and the newer Lac de Naussac (which he never knew), Auvergne cedes the trail to its principal host Lozère at the first major town, Langogne. The spectacular lonely Lozerien landscape begins with the easterm edge of the Margeride, granite and broom scrubland bringing light and shade to the green on the hills and gentle blues of the skies that seem closer than anywhere else. Stones by your feet begin to glisten - quicksilver trickles filtering out in all directions along grandest gorges to follow and become the powerful rivers of France.

The waters flow through a string of hamlets and villages weaving through werewolf land of Gevaudan: Legends to chill the night air and pastures to catch the sunshine breaking from the fruit-rich woods that festoon each fresh valley. Escape from the profane world of mythical beasts to the spiritual sanctuary of Our Lady of the Snows – a nudge away from La Bastide, and across the county border in the chestnut land of Ardèche.

From hills to mountains, Mont Lozère is burnished with heathers and the raiment of panorama. Look east to the Alps, west to the Pyrennees and, if your eyesight is a good as Stevenson's counsel, south to the Mediterranean. Stop here for a winter sports break late in the season, or grab the first culture fix of summer at le Pont de Montvert, where, just yards from the bridge of bloody memory, the many and varied talented artists of the Cevennes display and despatch their creations in a gallery shop. Draw closest to Stevenson here, where he truly felt the hand of history on his shoulder, and the stirrings of passion in his heart; come dine in the very room where he was tempted by the pulchritudious Clarisse.

Next: the second county town of Florac. And here the difference between north and south Lozère is understood. Unlike the orthodoxy of the land left behind, this is non-conformist country, where (rarity in France) protestant temples outnumber catholic churches, and the tradition of welcoming outsiders is never so vividly illustrated as on Thursday's market day when hippy market gardeners come to town selling their honeys, jams, and juices. Here the knife grinder sports a mohican crop and the farmer's wife a home made linen cap; young impoverished vignerons beg portions of garden for vines from landowners and pay their rent in bottles of wine; here artists open their studio doors onto the square. On any other day, find farm shops on the high street and musicians in shady squares. The boldest travellers undertaking the trek at Hallowe'en season, when many lodgings are closed for the winter, may warm themselves at the annual soup festival when the purchase of a ladle provides a weekend's sustenance.

Florac is gateway to the Cevennes, where grey lauze roof tiles, glimpsed through screens of chestnut and oak, gradually concede to the terracotta of the south, where empty cars parked by the roadside are the only sign of hunters and mushroom foragers tramping deep into autumn forests. In this land where once sheltered Huguenots and Camisards, and later Resistance fighters and Jews hid from more recent oppressors, the trail swoops from river beds to sunlit peaks, along the smoothed shelf of a lost railway, and eventually down to the substantial buildings of a proper town St Jean in the county of the Gard. The Latin Mediterranean begins here: Roman remains and bullfighting in Nîmes, forests surrendering territory to endless vineyards and the long promised heat of the Midi at last.

On the autumn weekend closest to Hallowe'en, a ladle strapped to your pack is passport to unlimited soup in Florac.

Getting There & Getting Around

Flying
Low cost airlines fly to Nîmes, Montpellier and Rodez. The local airport at Le Puy-Loudes is strictly domestic and Clermont Ferrand and St Etienne connect with French and continental cities. Within France, trains are usually quicker, cheaper and get you closer to your final destination. From outside France, Air France connects intercontinental flights with the TGV train to Nîmes from the station beneath Paris CDG Airport.

Air France www.airfrance.com
Easyjet easyjet.com
Ryanair www.ryanair.com
Clermont Ferrand Airport 04 73 62 71 00 www.clermont-aeroport.com
Montpellier Airport 04 67 20 85 00 www.montpellier.aeroport.fr
Nîmes Airport 04 66 70 49 49 www.nimes-aeroport.fr
Le Puy-en-Velay Airport 04 71 08 61 87
Rodez Airport 05 65 76 02 00
St-Etienne Airport 04 77 55 71 71 www.saint-etienne.aeroport.fr

Trains
By far the easiest way to travel to and through France: from UK, take Eurostar to Paris or Lille, and change to the excellent high-speed TGV national rail network. Within France, there are fast services to Clermont Ferrand and Nîmes, and you may also travel direct to Le Puy en Velay and Alès to top and tail the Stevenson Trail. Langogne is on the Paris-Clermont-Nîmes line. Through-ticketing from UK regions to your final destination. Bargain adance-booking options include internet-only IDTGV Paris-Nîmes from just €20 each way. First class upgrades are often inexpensive. Validate (*composter*) tickets in the orange or yellow franking machines before boarding. Disabled travellers see page 120.

SNCF (French National Rail Service)
08 92 35 35 35; www.voyages-sncf.com (in France)
Rail Europe www.raileurope.co.uk (UK); www.raileurope.com (US)

Crossing the Channel
Quickest and easiest option is Eurotunnel (**www.eurotunnel.com**), driving your car onto the train at Folkestone and off at Calais. Best value short Channel crossing from Dover is SpeedFerries fast service to Boulogne (**www.speedferries.com**). Norfolkline (**www.norfolkline.com**) offers cheap fares Dover-Dunkerque (but longer drive south). P&O (**www.poferries.com**) and SeaFrance (**www.seafrance.com**) run traditional ferries Dover-Calais.

Longer Western Channel crossings to Normandy and Brittany from Brittany Ferries (**www.brittanyferries.com**).

Driving

From Channel ports, go towards Paris to take the Périphérique round the capital and due south. **From Paris** *(allow 7 hours)*, head for Clermont Ferrand. **From Clermont Ferrand,** continue on the A75 to exit 20, then N102 to Le Puy en Velay. From Le Puy, the N88 and D38 lead to Le Monastier. **From the South** *(allow 3- 4 hours),* take the A75 to Clermont Ferrand, exit 20 (as above). **From Nîmes airport** *(allow 3.5 hours)*, take A54/A9/A7 leaving A7 exit 18, then N7/N102/N88. **From Rodez** (allow 3.5 hours), take N88 all the way to Le Puy (except for a 25km detour on the A75 until you come out of the Tunnel de Montjézieu).

Car Hire

Rental desks at most airports and stations. Best deals (with a no-excess guarantee) from **www.autoeurope.com** You may even collect a car in Auvergne and leave it at Alès or Nîmes at no extra charge.

Getting Around

On Foot

The GR70 trail is marked on trees and wooden posts with painted red and white stripes, indicating directions. Information from local rambling organisations (see page 181). Bring strong comfy shoes, warm and waterproof clothes for changeable weather and mountain nights, sunblock for exposed plateaux. Remember the country code: close gates, don't litter, no fires. Keep dogs on lead in national parks. Pack maps and GPS.

By Bike or Horse

Experienced riders and mountain-bikers should find most of the trail manageable, but there are four trickier stages, and you may wish to detour to main roads. The approach to Goudet is narrow and drops sharply. So too Mont Lozère to Finels. The track from Pont de Montvert to Bougès is steep, rocky and a very bumpy ride, and the final descent from the Col St Pierre just before St Jean du Gard is steep and narrow. Check hotel stabling optionsand facilities for bicycles.

Maps

The french **Topoguide Chemin Stevenson GR70** (FFRP - CHAMINA, ref. 700) has detailed maps of each stage. **IGN** maps: (scale 1: 100,000) 50 and 59 are ideal. Most detailed are **IGN** maps (scale 1: 25,000) 2735 E, 2736 E, 2737 E, 2738 E&O, 2739 OT, 2740 ET, 2741 ET, 2836 OT and 2840 OT.

Travelling with a Donkey

No need to haunt the cloisters of Le Puy nor yet accost a monk in the market place at Le Monastier. These days, a donkey-hire cottage industry has grown up along the trail, supplying beasts of burden to wayfarers

Learn a lesson or two from RLS – remember to "poot" and not to be tricked off-course by your four legged companion. But certainly do not follow his example of beating the beast into submission nor overwork her with too long a walk. Understand that a 40-kilo load is ample for any donkey, so, unlike our illustrious predecessor, leave the heavy eggwhisk at home and pack sensibly. All donkeys for hire on the route will know the paths by heart and be used to the ways of green drivers, but each is a little individual and will have its own foibles. When choosing your donkey, do not be afraid to ask questions of its owner – does it get on well with dogs, for instance? From Stevenson, you'll know that a donkey travels at its own pace, most comfortably at around 3kph. So relax and enjoy the view. Allow for interruptions as passers by will want to stop and take photos!

In truth, you will be introduced to your new travel mate, and taught the basics of handling, driving, grooming and feeding. Allow up to 2 hours for training on Day One. You will also be given a user's manual!

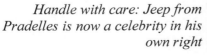 Do plan ahead when travelling with a donkey. Hotels, guesthouses, and restaurants on the trail that offer a welcome to donkeys are marked in the listing section of this guide with the carrot symbol (left).

Handle with care: Jeep from Pradelles is now a celebrity in his own right

But remember, whilst all provide a paddock or somewhere to tether your charge safely overnight, not every establishment will offer to feed the donkey. So make sure you've enough fodder with you and check where to get more supplies if needed. Your donkey will munch on leaves, grass and hedges during the day, but will need a good kilo of barley or prepared feed each evening and a half portion again for breakfast. The **Fédération Nationale Anes et Randonnée** has lots of useful information at **www.ane-et-rando.com** with detailed and very readable English language advice.

Budget from €30-50 per day, and upwards of €200 for a week's rental and remember that, unless making a round trip, the cost of returning the donkey by van at the end of your stay adds anything from €40-300. Pay around €500 for a full 12-day one-way donkey hire including collection. Some owners might also offer you a lift back to the starting point if you've a car to pick-up, or they may drive your own vehicle down meet you.

The **Association Stevenson** (see page 181) recommends the following addresses along the trail for renting a donkey. They can deliver the animal to your own starting point. All offer advice and suggestions on donkey friendly establishments en route.

Les Anes à Gilles Rocher de Grelet, 43420 Pradelles
04 66 69 49 35;
mobile 06 81 60 76 58
www.lesanesagilles.com
Gilles Romand is himself a familiar figure on the trail, his horseboxes dropping off and collecting his donkeys. Each of his animals has its own webpage on Gilles' site and past travelling companions email their former Modestines. Jeep is a media savvy celebrity in his own right having appeared on TV and in many magazine articles

Gentiâne
Castagnoles, 48220 Vialas
04 66 41 04 16
http://anegentil.free.fr

Rando-Ane
4 route du Monastier,
43700 Arsac-en-Velay
04 71 03 99 31;
mobile 06 86 81 73 19
www.bourricot.com

Badjane
Cessénades, 30450
Malons-et-Elze
04 66 56 71 54;
www.badjane.org

Onagre
Station du Mont-Lozère,
48190 Cubières;
& Bousségures,
48110 St Martin de Lanuscle
04 66 48 66 10;
mobile: 06 86 73 21 14
asso-onagre@wanadoo.fr

Public Transport

There is no public transport alternative to the complete Stevenson route, but you may still visit around a dozen key destinations by bus or train. And more than half the walking distance can be swapped for a comfy seat on a bus or train with canny juggling of timetables.

Regular train services run from Le Puy en Velay to Langogne (50 min) and from La Bastide-St-Laurent (2 hours) and Alès (35 min) to Nîmes, You may sample the actual single track railway line planned by RLS's dining companions at Chasseradès: trains alternate with a bus service for the 12-minute journey from La Bastide. Within the area itself, trains stop at very few local stations, but the railways run a daily summer shuttle bus between Le Puy en Velay and Pradelles (around 35 min) and on to Langogne (another 15 min). Another railway shuttle coach runs from Langogne to Luc (around 20 min) and La Bastide-St-Laurent (another 10 min) several times a day.

A network of local buses link several villages and towns. Anyone may use these services, which usually run around the school timetable. Bus 46 from Le Puy to Le Monastier takes 40 minutes, leaving at 9 in the morning (Mon), 12.25 (Wed) and 18.15 (Mon, Tue, Thu and Fri) - school terms only. Bus number 1 links Le Puy en Velay to Landos (around 35 min) and Langogne (another 20 min). Up to three services Mon-Fri, year round.

No bus connection between the northern and southern sections of the route. So Chasserades to Florac is strictly for hikers or motorists – but for many, this the best section of the walking route in any case! Nonetheless, once you reach the southern half of the trail, a bus from Florac leaves the former railway station at 9am daily (Mon-Sat, year round), stopping at St Julien d'Arpaon (9.10) and Cassagnas (9.18), and arriving at Alés at 10.15. Even RLS himself opted for public transport at the end of the journey. No stage coaches these days, but you may hop on the number 40 bus from St Jean de Gard to Nîmes. There are several buses a day (just 2 in summer holidays). Journey time 1hour 15 minutes.

Most local bus services run during school term time only (unless specified). There are no services at all on Sundays nor on public holidays. Do check before travelling since timetables and services are always subject to change or cancellation. You might prefer to begin your excursions at Langogne or La Bastide, but remember, public transport options are available from the very beginning.

Le Monastier – Le Puy *(bus)*

Le Puy – Landos or **Pradelles - Langogne** *(Bus):* Stay in Langogne or take a day or two off-route by the lakes.

Langogne – Luc *(bus):* Perhaps walk from here to Cheylard l'Evêque for an overnight treat in a chambre d'hôte or gîte.

Luc – La Bastide *(bus):* Overnight here or perhaps walk to the monastery of Notre Dame des Neiges across the county border in Ardèche.

La Bastide – Chasseradès *(train or bus):* Overnight at a hikers' hotel or guesthouse and enjoy hearty country cooking to prepare for a proper walk the next day as this is the end of the line for public transport for the next 60km or so. From here, you may either return to La Bastide and take the train to Alés or Nîmes, or a taxi through to Florac, or, since this is for many walkers the dramatic highlight of the route, taking in the evocative sites including Pont de Monvert, why not make this section of the itinerary your main hiking holiday, and enjoy the magnificent ridge walk towards Florac with the breathtaking views that inspired some of Stevenson's most glorious prose.

Florac - St Julien d'Arpaon or **Cassagnas** *(bus):* A relatively gentle stretch of the walk uses an abandoned railway line.

St Julien d'Arpaon or **Cassagnas - Alés** *(bus):* You can leave now and skip the rest of the trail, just catch the Alés bus. But with just 35km walking left to walk, or one more overnight between here at St Jean du Gard, why not travel on foor just as far as your hero under the open skies.

St Jean de Gard – Nîmes *(bus)* or **Alés –Nîmes** *(train):* Remember, a purist would certainly take public transport for the last few miles!

Information

Trains and railway bus services www.voyages-sncf.com 08 92 35 35 35
Le Puy - Le Monastier www.cg43.fr 04 71 03 85 80
Le Puy - Langogne www.cg43.fr 04 66 49 03 81
Florac-Ales www.ville-florac.fr/transports.htm 04 66 45 00 18
St Jean - Ales www.coopcar.fr 04 66 52 01 45

Taxi
Stevenson Bagages 04 66 47 04 66; mobile 06 07 29 01 23
www.stevenson-bagages.com

Disabled Travellers

The Route

Since the Stevenson Trail passes through a good many towns and villages, the route is punctuated by various entry points and one may choose stretches of the route best suited to individual mobility. The easiest and flattest section comes after Florac, between St Julien d'Arpaon and Cassagnas – the 7.7 km path here is a former railway line and therefore level for use by most wheelchairs. A shorter stretch along a plateau from Le Bouchet St Nicolas goes towards Landos, but its final couple of kilometres are rougher, and you may prefer to turn back to Le Bouchet. The Association Stevenson (see page 181) can advise on options according to specific mobility – selecting portions of the trail for hikers with sticks and rollators, or users of sports wheelchairs. Travelling by car, you may cherry-pick sites and stretches of the full itinerary and an encouraging number of establishments en route are recognising that they have an obligation to welcome guests of differing levels of mobility (page 122).

Transport

Crossing the Channel

Ferry and channel tunnel operators are very helpful. **Speedferries** and **Brittany Ferries** (see page 114) can arrange for your car to be parked onboard near flat, wheelchair access to the passenger lounge. Just check in an hour before your crossing. **Eurotunnel** is the easiest option of all as you do not need to leave the car during the 35 minute crossing. Onboard wc is not wheelchair accessible, so use facilities at the terminal before departure.

Flying

Let airlines know special requirements at the time of booking. **Le Puy** airport is least practical, with flights from Paris only. The train link is easier (see below). The airport is wheelchair accessible with suitable wcs, but no dedicated boarding service. **Rodez** and **Nîmes** airports are accessible, providing assistance boarding and disembarking and adapted wcs. **Clermont Ferrand** and **Montpellier** airports are fully accessible with specialist welcome/boarding service and well-designed toilet facilities.

Trains

Since there is no direct rail service to the starting point of the Stevenson Trail, travellers from Paris should book the train from Paris Gare de Lyon to Le Puy en Velay, changing at Clermont Ferrand (since this is the only route with assistance throughout the journey). The return trip from Nîmes is direct, with no changes. Travelling from UK, remember that Eurostar arrives in Paris at Gare du Nord, and you'll have to cross the city by taxi to get to Gare de Lyon. Best options from UK: Eurostar from London to Lille, then simply change platforms for the TGV to Nîmes. Summer Saturdays only: Eurostar from London to Avignon, where you may pick up local trains to Nîmes and Alès.

A 19th century railway system, with underpasses, staircases and sometimes three or four steep steps between platform and train has often proved inaccessible. Smaller country stations remain impractical for mobility-restricted travellers. However, six key stations for access to the Stevenson route from the outside world now offer a full support system for disabled travellers with a dedicated team providing a comprehensive range of specialist assistance accessing platforms, boarding trains and journey planning. Available free of charge to disabled travellers at

| **Clermont-Ferrand** | **Mende** | **Nîmes** |
| **Le Puy en Velay** | **Alès** | **Montpellier** |

Service Accès Plus
0890 640 650 (then press 1) from France only
accesplus@sncf.fr; www.accesplus.sncf.com
Office hours 7am-10pm
Contact Acces Plus at least 48 hours before travelling to arrange assistance. Advisors can also help plan your journey in advance and suggest alternative routes and facilities. Arrive at the station 30 minutes before departure to be accompanied all the way to reserved seats on the train. The train manager will be informed as to your needs, and a team member waiting for at your destination. If your train is delayed or journey disrupted, call the helpline from your mobile phone on **0890 640 650** (then press **2**). Passengers with hearing disabilities can text on **06 10 64 06 50**.

Buses
French buses are traditional touring coaches with several steep steps and not adapted to the needs of disabled passengers.

Driving
Blue badges issued in any EU country may be used in France.

Planning a trip
The national tourist office website has the usual info: **www.franceguide.com** then follow links **Practical Information > During Your Stay > France for Disabled People**. Contact départemental tourist offices (see page 181) and ask for the *Tourisme et Handicap* brochure or listings.

Accommodation

France has embraced the concept of accessibility with enthusiasm, if not always with the most practical of approaches. One hotel, for example, has adapted a bedroom with ensuite to the utmost – the only problem is that there is no level wheelchair access into the building itself! However, other venues go beyond expectations. Not only are the bathrooms in the "accessible" apartments at the Cap Défi sports centre perfectly arranged for wheelchair users, but you can slide under kitchen worksurfaces for cooking and washing up, the café bar downstairs is fully welcoming and even the sailing boats outside are set up for chair users.

In reality, several hotels have ground-floor accommodation, if not all with universally practical bathrooms. Many campsites and self catering units have shower and toilet facilities fully tailored for wheelchair users. In the listings pages, whenever "disabled" facilities are limited, we point this out, since some establishments are more geared to modest mobility restrictions. Nonetheless, do telephone ahead to check on your specific needs

Le Puy en Valay
Hotel Capucins

Le Monastier
Auberge des Acacias
Moulin de Savin (campsite)

Bouchet St Nicolas!
l'Arrestadou
Gîte d'Etape Communal

Landos
Les Fonds (gîte d'étape)

Langogne
Domaine des Barres
Terrasses du Lac
Cap Defi (gîtes)

Bastide PuyLaurent
Grande Halte
Allier (campsite)

Chasserades
Les Sources
Le Mirandol (gîte d'étape)

Le Bleymard
Les Alpiers
La Combette
La gazelle (campsite)

Bédouès
Chantemerle (campsite)
Chon du Tarn (campsite)

Mont Lozère
Le Refuge

Florac
Grand Hotel du Parc
Val Village des Vacances
Pont du Tarn (campsite)

Saint Jean du Gard
Les Belluges

Follow the Stevenson Trail by Car

By car, the journey from Le Puy en Velay to Alès runs to around 300km. The route below does not follow the precise GR70 trail, but it does allow you to see the sites in the same order as RLS purists. The road route is useful compromise for mixed parties, allowing hikers and motorists to meet up each night at a designated hotel, with luggage safely transported by car. Travellers with restricted mobility (see page 120), may combine a motoring holiday with the opportunity to pick up the GR70 at such spots as Landos and Cassagnas.

The route

From **Le Puy**, follow the N88/D38 to **Le Monastier-sur-Gazeille**, where Stevenson set off on foot. From Le Monastier, pick up the D500 initally called the route du Pont de l'Estaing and take the D49 through **Goudet** then the D311 to **Bouchet St Nicolas**. The D31/D53/D88 will lead you to **Landos**. Then take the D52 and the N88 which runs through **Pradelles, Langogne** and **Chaudeyrac**.

At Chaudeyrac, take the D206 to **Cheylard l'Evêque**, D71 to **Luc** and then the D906/D4 to **St Laurent les Bains** (*via La Bastide*). The abbey is reached via a long driveway. Return on the D4 to **La Bastide Puylaurent**, then follow the D6 route de Mende until you get to **Chasseradès**.

From **Chasseradès**, keep to the D6/D120 until **Le Bleymard**. Nest, the D20 to **Mas d'Orcieres**. And stay on the same road to reach **Finels** and **Le Pont de Montvert**. From here, you may either elect to take the D20 to **Mijavols** or follow the D998 to **Cocurès** and **Bédouès**. Continue along the D998 then turn left onto the main N106 to **Florac**.

If you decide to leave the trail here, the Corniche des Cevennes is a stunning drive to St Jean du Gard, but otherwise, to continue with the Stevenson tour, leave town on the rue Théophile Roussel then the N106 to **St Julien d'Arpaon** and on to **Cassagnas**. From here, choose the D62/D162/D13, following signs for **St Martin de Lansucle**. Then join the D28/D13 to St **Germain de Calberte**. D984 through **St Etienne Vallée Française** then D983 to **St Jean du Gard**.

To continue to the end of the line, leave St Jean du Gard on the avenue Abraham Mazel and follow the meandering D50 to **Mialet** and **Alès**.

Accommodation

Like Stevenson, you may have invested in a sleeping bag and a couple of loaves of dry bread. However, the option of freshly-laundered sheets, fluffy bathrowels and the prospect of a hearty home-cooked meal could well keep you from the great outdoors and at one with your own creature comforts.

Considering that the 250km of the GR70 path has managed to avoid the scars of the modern tourist industry, and that none of the big national chain hotels are anywhere to be found throughout the entire county of Lozère, there is a true wealth of accommodation to choose from along the trail.

In some towns and villages you will find the same dilemma: a couple of inns or small hotels, a gîte or hostel or two, maybe a cosy guesthouse offering table d'hôte dining. Perhaps even a welcome at the local monastery. All provide accommodation for travellers and an overnight welcome to a donkey. In other villages or hamlets, no choice: just the one establishment or the reality of walking another 5 or 10km. So plot your journey carefully if you wish to overnight within your own comfort zone.

In larger towns, you may find the occasional 3-star hotel for unashamed truancy from the past. Many 1 and 2 star establishments will be family-run Logis, graded with 1-3 *cheminée* logos. Other traditional coashing inns could date from Stevenson's day. And an hotel will usually have a restaurant with a choice of menus to suit mood and budget.

Chambre d'hôte is France's take on B&B, and often even better than an hotel. Stay in a private home or farmhouse, perhaps dining *en famille* or with other guests from a set menu.

Self catering in gîtes or bunking down in hostels offer good value for money (you'll need to use your sleeping bag or bring your own sheets - see page 142). The budget option – in summer – is the local campsite, where you may overnight for just a few euros and you might refresh yourself with either a shower or a dip in the river.

A few holiday centres in park or lakeland and the occasional grander hotel (maybe even with a golf course) provide delightful distractions to the hike at hand before returning to the trail, setting the pedometer back to zero and making those "pooting" noises to get your donkey back on track.

Hotels

Symbols

R	Room only
HB	Half board (dinner, bed and breakfast)
€	under 35 euros
€€	35 – 50 euros
€€€	over 50 euros
* -***	Official star rating

 Donkeys welcome

 Dogs welcome

Le Puy en Velay

Appart'Hotel des Capucins**
43000 Le Puy en Velay
04 71 04 23 74
contact@le-puy.de; www.le-puy.de
R: €€€

For weary rail travellers straight off the train, or disabled guests seeking a decent and fully adapted hotel room (the efficiently German run Capucins is well used to welcoming mobility-restricted guests), an address within 10 minutes of the station is an overnight stop for travellers too exhausted to make it to Stevenson's starting point at Le Monastier. Book a room, a flat or a gîte d'étape stay.

Le Monastier sur Gazeille

Auberge des Acacias
1 Rond-Point des Acacias, 43150 Le Monastier sur Gazeille
04 71 08 38 11
auberge.lesacacias@wanadoo.fr; www.auberge-pays-auvergne.com/auberge_acacias.htm
R: €€   HB: €€

Just four bedrooms, each individually decorated and with a name instead of a number. The restaurant serves traditional local fare. Wheelchair aceess to restaurant only.

Le Provence **
Av des Ecoles, 43150 Le Monastier sur Gazeille
04 71 03 82 37
leprovence.lemonastier@wanadoo.fr; www.le-provence.com
R: €€   HB: €€
See page 163

Goudet

La Loire
Le Bourg, 43150 Goudet
04 71 57 18 41
hoteldelaloire.goudet@wanadoo.fr; www.hotel-de-la-loire-goudet.com
Closed: mid-Nov - Mar
R: €€

An imposing traditional stone building in the heart of the village, with wide arched windows looking out to the street and the terrace, and flooding the dining room with sunlight. 21 bedrooms upstairs and the main restaurant and bar of Goudet on the ground floor. Don't do a Stevenson and hurry too swiftly over the midday meal. Take your time. And don't forget the camera – you'll want to record the stunning views of the Chateau Beaufort perched precariously on its rocky tower before you leave.

Langogne

Domaine de Barres ***
Route de Mende, 48300 Langogne
04 66 46 08 37; Fax 04 66 46 23 42
domainedebarres@yahoo.fr; www.domainedebarres.com
R: €€€ HB: €€€

Not on the Relais Stevenson list, this golf club hotel and restaurant is the slightly more luxe (well, 3-star) option. Access to the restaurant and main public areas for wheelchair users, and a lift to the bedrooms. Rooms are spacious enough for disabled guests, but bathrooms not adapted for a wheelchair. Special all inclusive rates including green fees. Dogs welcome at a €20 daily supplement. Full review see page 165.

Le Grill du Gaillard **

Quartier du Pont d'Allier, 48300 Langogne
04 66 69 10 55
R: €€   HB: €€
Gaze out at the river Allier from the restaurant of the old-fashioned Hôtel Gaillard. A big field for the donkeys and 17 bedrooms for the rest of us.

Les Terrasses du Lac

48300 Langogne
04 66 69 29 62
info@naussac.com; www.naussac.com
Closed: Nov-Mar
R: €€   HB: €€
If you don't have a breathtaking view of the lake from your bedroom window, then you'll probably look out over the equally calming sight of cows grazing contentedly in a nearby field. One of several out of town options for the Langogne stopover situated around the man made lake of Naussac that flooded the original eponymous village. The church steeple was rescued from the underwater village and now stands by a modern church on the waters' edge. The hotel and campsite has a restaurant with superb lake panoramas. Half-board includes buffet breakfast and a choice of 3-course dinner menus. Self-catering chalets and a campsite (with swimming pool) offer alternatives to the hotel comforts. Ideal base for an active detour with watersports and plenty of other outdoor activities from cycling and canoeing to potholing and sailing, for those who find that a donkey alone does not pump up the adrenaline. Wifi internet access for travellers who need to keep one hand holding on to real life. A ground-floor room is fitted for disabled guests.

Chaudeyrac

Hôtel-Restaurant de France**

Route de la Clamouse, 48170 Chaudeyrac
04 66 47 91 00; fax: 04.66.47.93.29
tremoulet.yves@wanadoo.fr; www.hotel-lozere.net
R: €€   HB: €€
A practical overnight stop on the route where for just 4 euros guests may upgrade from the half-board menu in the restaurant to the full menu de terroir – aligot, charcuterie and of course mushrooms in season. Since the hotel is more than a mile from the route proper, hikers on the Stevenson

trail should call the Tremoulet family in advance to arrange for a free transfer from Cheylard l'Evêque and Chaudeyrac.

Bastide – Puylaurent

La Grande Halte *
rue des Tilleuls, 48250 La Bastide - Puylaurent
04 66 46 00 35
Closed Nov-Mar
R: €€€ HB: €€

Weary travellers have long been a familiar sight at the door of La Grande Halte, which has welcomed overnighters since the days of stagecoaches passing through en route to Nîmes and Clermont Ferrand and then continued the tradition of hospitality with the coming of the railways. There are 20 rooms, one of which is suitable for a family of up to 12. One ground floor bedroom can accommodate guests with some disabilities, although the bathroom is not yet equipped for a wheelchair. Level access to the restaurant and bar.

Les Genêts
rue des Tilleuls, 48250 La Bastide - Puylaurent
04 66 46 00 13
hotelgenets@yahoo.fr
Closed early-Nov - mid-April
R: €   HB: €

Lower priced neighbouring option is this restaurant, hotel and bar in the heart of La Bastide-Puylaurent, with a choice of regional menus.

Chasseradès

Les Sources
48250 Chasseradès
04 66 46 01 14
Closed: Nov-Feb
HB: €€
Just outside the village, a genuine welcome from a true enthusiast of the Stevenson trail. Modest supplement for donkeys. See review page 168.

128

Le Bleymard

La Remise **

48190 Le Bleymard
04 66 48 65 80; Fax : 04 66 48 63 70
contact@hotel-laremise.com; www.hotel-laremise.com
Closed mid-Dec - Jan
R: €€   HB: €€

Mine hosts at this old stage-post on the main road through the village know how to look after their guests, and enter into the spirit of the Stevenson trail, yet such is their genial welcome they might well find themselves accused of delaying the itinerant traveller to bide a while longer. Sure, there is a paddock for the donkeys, but, once the beasts of burden are settled in, Claude and Jean-François are more than happy to show guests the many other attractions of Lozère. Fly fishing is among passions catered for, with even fly-making workshops on the agenda. As are well-being breaks with physical stretching and breathing excercises, and adrelenine-pumping motor bike trails and itineraries.

Rooms are simple, tasteful and smart. Just the sort of place for which you cross fingers when you see a listing marked with 2 "cheminées" in the Logis de France guide. The Logis tradition of "terroir", good honest local food, is certainly respected here. Traditional recipes as old as the stone walls and wooden beams of the inn, are presented in a contemporary style on a smart plate. A 17-euro menu features the Cevenol speciality truffade (cheese and potato cake with bacon) and the Bleymard take on the ubiquitous Salade Stevenson (variants on the theme can be discovered the length of the trail and invariably include such regional produce as bleu de pays cheese, walnuts and chestnuts and ham).

Mont Lozère (Ski Resort)

Le Montlo

48190 Mas d'Orcières, Station du Mont Lozère
04 66 45 81 30
info@lemontlo.com; www.montlo.com
HB: €€

Popular with school parties (rooms sleep 2-10 guests) for winter sports breaks, the hotel is well enough equipped to deal with families: not only table football, ping-pong, pool and darts, but ski and outdoor sports kit for hire. The hotel also has its own roller skating rink. Accommodation charged per person rather than per room. Accommodation only from around the €20 euro mark. Lively dinners at 1400 metres above sea level!

Le Refuge **

48190 Mas d'Orcières, Station du Mont Lozère
04 66 48 62 83
guylene.frouin@orange.fr; http://vacances-cevennes-lozere.com
Closed: Nov
R: €€   HB: €€
A relatively modern winter-sports-resort hotel with all the off-season comforts. Warm your hands, your toes and your labrador in front of an open fire in the bar, indulge in a family fondue in the dining room and even hire ski equipment for a day on the piste. Lovely views of the slopes from the terrace. Hospitable welcome from hosts Guylène et Michel. Both hotel and restaurant are accessible to guests with restricted mobility.

Pont de Montvert

Auberge des Cévennes

48220 Le Pont de Montvert
04 66 45 80 01
Closed: mid-Nov – mid-Mar
R: €   HB: €€
One of Stevenson's original stopovers, where he was wined, dined and even wooed and nearly won. See pages 72 for the story and 169 for lunch.

Aux Sources du Tarn **

48220 Le Pont de Montvert
04 66 45 80 25
auxsourcesdutarn@wanadoo.fr, www.hotellozere.com
R: €€   HB: €€€
Simple rooms with ensuite facilities, a restaurant serving Bernard Mazoyer's regionally sourced meat and fish dishes and a summer dining terrace overlooking the river Tarn itself.

Cocurès

La Lozerette **

48400 Cocurès
04 66 45 06 04

Stevenson's Auberge des Cévenes still standing by the River Tarn

lalozerette@wanadoo.fr; www.lalozerette.com
Closed: Nov - Easter
R: €€€   HB: €€€
Truly welcoming hotel with very well-respected dining room and wine list.
See full review page 171.

Florac

Grand Hôtel du Parc ***
47 avenue Jean Monestier, 48400 Florac
04 66 45 03 05
grand-hotel-du-parc@wanadoo.fr; www.grandhotelduparc.fr
Closed: mid-Nov-Mar
R: €€   HB: €€-€€€

The major three-star hotel of this bustling and vibrant market town of
Florac. Bedrooms are smart or pretty and have views of the wooded
grounds or the mountains. A swimming pool in the gardens. Summer
lunches are served on the terrace and year-round dining in the restaurant.
Although local listings boast that the hotel has a bedroom designed for
mobility restricted guests, be aware that there are nonetheless still a
number of steps to negotiate in order to enter the building.

Hotel des Gorges du Tarn **
48 rue du Pêcher, 48400 Florac
04 66 45 00 63; fax: 04 66 45 10 56
gorges-du-tarn.adonis@wanadoo.fr; www.hotel-gorgesdutarn.com
Closed Nov-Easter (restaurant closed Wed except Jul-Aug)
R: €€ - €€€   HB: €€ - €€€
Not officially on the Stevenson circuit, but perfectly located for the trail,
with town-centre parking for travellers without four-legged companions.
This is a seriously top-end Logis de France hotel and restaurant. Bedrooms
are in the main building and a modern annexe just behind the restaurant.
Committed refitting of the rooms in 2008 is creating a truly smart and
comfortable modern space, with some stylish ideas in the décor of the
annexe rooms. Lovely use of colour and soft furnishings, some rooms have
a sofa for relaxing in peace and quiet. Bedrooms in the main building
already have wifi access, which is also available in the reception area
where, on my last visit, we enjoyed an exhibition of amusing sculptures.
Lovely friendly staff and a very agreeable restaurant l'Adonis – see review
page 172.

Saint Jean du Gard

Hotel de l'Oronge **
103 Grand rue, place de la Révolution, 30270 St Jean du Gard
04 66 85 30 34; fax: 04 66 85 39 73
oronge@wanadoo.fr; www.loronge.com
R: €€   HB: €€€
Relive Stevenson's farewell to Modestine at this old stage post at the end
of his original walk. See review page 177.

Les Bellugues **

13 rue Pelet de la Lozère, 30270 Saint Jean du Gard
04 66 85 15 33; fax: 04 66 85 32 08
hotelbellugues@wanadoo.fr; www.hotel-bellugues.com
Closed: mid-Nov – mid-Mar
R: €€€
A touch of the exotic in the setting of a former silkworks at the heart of
town. A bamboo and palm tree garden around a heated swimming pool is
nicely indulgent for relaxing after two weeks on the road. The welcome is
warm and friendly. Rooms are tastefully simple and comfortable.
Independent restaurant next door. Room for wheelchair users on the
ground floor.

Alès

Hôtel Durand **
3, Boulevard Anatole France, 30100 Alès
04 66 86 28 94
dorel.nowacki@orange.fr; www.hotel-durand.fr
R: €€
The pun in the name of the town Alès (the more modern spelling than that
adopted by the Scots writer of the nineteenth century) lies in its suggestion
of relaxation and ease at the end of a long journey. The Stevenson people
suggest this stop over as convenient for the railway station less than 100
yards away. Recently modernised rooms are basic, but clean and with
ensuite facilities, and the welcome is cheerful and genuine. Despite the
suggestion in some guides that there are rooms equipped for the disabled,
this is not quite the case, but the friendly reception staff will do their best
to provide a ground floor room for guests with restricted mobility if you
book in advance. Rooms from under 40 euros.

Chambres d'Hôtes

Symbols

R   Room only
HB   Half board (dinner, bed and breakfast)
€   under 35 euros
€€   35 – 50 euros
€€€ over 50 euros
* -*** Official tourist office rating

 Donkeys welcome

 Dogs welcome

Le Monastier sur Gazeille

Blaisine et Philomène ***
50 rue St Pierre, 43250 Le Monastier sur Gazeille
04 71 03 80 26
elisabeth.chalindar@wanadoo.fr; http://perso.orange.fr/blaisine
Open year round, but reservation essential Oct-Mar
R: €

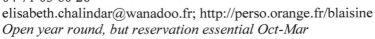

Elisabeth Chalidar's cosy guesthouse is her own home. She has two double rooms and a triple on offer at her house in the village and has long waved off intrepid hikers on their pilgrimages towards the Cevennes. No dining option, just breakfast, but Elisabeth can advise on where to eat in the village, whether you fancy the full meal at the Acacias, Moulin or Provence or perhaps just a simple pizza at Lou Pizzicato along the road from the house.

Le Bouchet Saint Nicolas

L'Arrestadou ***
Chambres d'hôtes & ferme-auberge
Route de Cayres, 43510 Le Bouchet Saint Nicolas
04 71 57 35 34

larrestadou@wanadoo.fr; www.larrestadou.com
Closed: mid-Nov – mid-Feb
R: €€   HB: €

Now this is what I call country life. If you opt to overnight chez la famille Villeseche, you many choose either to stay in the village or to spend the night in a farm building down on the land. The doors of the ferme-auberge cabin style rooms open out onto the fields where safely graze Montbelliard cows and Noir de Velay black sheep. The blue room has been designed for guests with physical disabilities, sleeping 3 on the ground floor and a further two in the mezzanine. Two more rooms available out here and a couple more in the village house. Dine well, the terrines, tarts and recipes from the farmer's kitchen showcase home-reared meats, wild berries and mushrooms from the surrounding countryside and the breakfast dairy produce started as a moo outside your bedroom window.

Chez Andrée et Augustin Reynaud ***

Chambres & table d'hôtes
43510 Le Bouchet Saint Nicolas
04 71 57 31 91
Closed: Nov-Mar
R: €€   HB: €

If you seek the famous puy lentils come of Auvergne, then look no further than your plate. World-class pulses are the very farm produce served in many guises at every meal at the chambre d'hôte near the Lac du Bouchet.

Langogne

Le Modest'inn *

Chambres & table d'hôtes
2 rue de la Honde, 48300 Langogne
06 07 61 55 66
philippe.blanc@gr70.com; www.gr70.com/chambres.htm
R: €€

Oh how the French love their puns, bless 'em. And words play their part in this appropriately modest B&B (no ensuites, so bring slippers and jim-jams) as the house has a cosy little library where you may browse the literary reflections of those who have passed this way before you. Other guests might squander an hour around the pool table. The place is being renovated with green credentials. The house speciality aligot is served to table d'hôte diners, and wise counsel on alternative dining options freely shared. François Bouyon's restaurant at nearby Gevaudan recommended by your host Philippe Blanc as a worthy detour for wine lovers.

Cheylard l'Évêque

Le Refuge du Moure ***
Chambres & table d'hôtes
48300 Cheylard l'Évêque
04 66 69 03 21
info@lozere-gite.com; www.lozere-gite.com
Closed: Nov-Mar; first week in July
R: €€€ HB: €€

The quaint décor is one thing, the gorgeous cooking aromas another. Prepare to be wooed and won by this delightful guesthouse. See review page 167.

La Bastide-Puylaurent

L'Etoile
Chambres & tables d'hôte and gîte d'étape
route de Mende, 48250 La Bastide-Puylaurent
04 66 46 05 52
papadimitriou4@hotmail.com; www.etoile.fr
Closed mid-May – mid-Sep
HB: €€

Philippe Papadimitriou discovered this place back in 1991. It was a sad run-down shadow of the once fashionable hotel that had welcomed Riviera escapees in the long hot summers before the War. Undaunted (after all, his family once owned the Hotel de Paris in Cairo), he set about restoring the place as a cheerful guesthouse. It may not be in the official Stevenson listings, still, with chambre d'hôte, gîte d'étape and even camping options in the grounds, the convivial Etoile comes to life each summer. Five-course dinner at 7.30 is a taste of the trail, featuring cheeses from Luc and the wine of Notre Dame des Nieges, rounded off with verbena tea from Le Puy. Conviviality spills over to the piano bar, and night owls have until 9.30 the next morning to grab breakfast, with home made bread and jam. Six of the 16 rooms have ensuite facilities. When booking, ask if you may leave your car at the hotel for a few days as you hit the trail.

Chasseradès

Le Relais de Modestine
Chambres & table d'hôtes
48250 Chasseradès
04 66 46 29 16; mobile 06 69 52 75 90
contact@stevenson-en-cevennes.fr; www.stevenson-en-cevennes.fr
R: €€   HB: €€€

From the street this looks just like a smart modern restaurant in the centre of the village. But beyond the tables of the dining room, this well renovated house has five very individually and tastefully styled rooms. Each gently themed bedroom has an ensuite bath or shower room. Ghislaine (or Gigi to her family) and Patrice Surget and their children welcome guests year round.

Le Bleymard

Les Alpiers
Chambres & table d'hôtes
48190 Le Bleymard
04 66 48 67 19
pedibuslozere@wanadoo.fr; www.randonnee-lozere.com
Closed Nov-Mar
HB: €€

Madame Abenque used to run a Logis de France hotel and restaurant, so there is a lifetime of professionalism behind the friendly welcome at this traditional travellers' lodge. Arrive by bike, on foot, on horseback or with a donkey and be assured of a welcome. Simple cabin style rooms have four beds and ensuite showers. Disabled guests are well catered for and the lodge has a lift. Breakfast and dinner are served against a panoramic backdrop of Le Mont Lozère.

La Combette ***
Chambres & table d'hôtes
48190 Saint Jean du Bleymard
04 66 48 61 35; Fax: 04 66 48 61 36
lacombette@wanadoo.fr; www.lacombette.com; cevennes-mont-lozere.com
R: €€€ HB: €€

A welcome drink awaits arrivals at La Combette. Chambres d'hôtes in a smart house at the heart of a cluster of alternative self catering accommodation from a contemporary designed gîte to holiday chalets. Home cooking for overnight guests in the main house. One chalet has been designed to welcome disabled guests and their families. Free internet.

L'Escoutal **

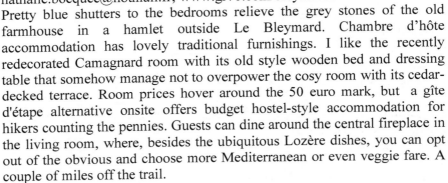

Chambres & table d'hôtes
Hameau du Bonnetès, 48190 Le Bleymard
04 66 48 64 08; mobile 06 78 27 12 97
R: €€€ HB: €€
nathalie.bocquee@hotmail.fr; www.gr70.com/bleymard.htm
Pretty blue shutters to the bedrooms relieve the grey stones of the old farmhouse in a hamlet outside Le Bleymard. Chambre d'hôte accommodation has lovely traditional furnishings. I like the recently redecorated Camagnard room with its old style wooden bed and dressing table that somehow manage not to overpower the cosy room with its cedar-decked terrace. Room prices hover around the 50 euro mark, but a gîte d'étape alternative onsite offers budget hostel-style accommodation for hikers counting the pennies. Guests can dine around the central fireplace in the living room, where, besides the ubiquitous Lozère dishes, you can opt out of the obvious and choose more Mediterranean or even veggie fare. A couple of miles off the trail.

Le Pont de Montvert / Finiels

Maison Victoire ***

Chambres & table d'hôtes
Hameau de Finiels
48220, Le Pont de Montvert
04 66 45 84 36
jacqueline.galzin@free.fr; www.gites-mont-lozere.com
HB: €€
Why did the chicken cross the road? Because we had just driven up to the stone archway of the Maison Victoire at Finiels. Hens scurrying into the hedges, sheep grazing in the fields – three cheers for the timelessness of village life that turned back watches and body clocks as soon as we entered the hamlet. It had been six long years since last I had chewed the fat with Jaccqueline and Mario at their cheery B&B overlooking the lush southern slopes of the Mont Lozère and just 5km from the seminal stopover of Le

Pont de Montvert. As we wandered over to the courtyard in front of the house, there they were, still shelling beans and sorting fruits destined for home made tarts and jams into boxes, buckets and baskets around the old stone table where evening guests would soon sit to gaze across the valley.

Pies and preserves are not the only home made speciality of the house, the rebuilding of the Maison Victoire is a labour of love in itself. The main room on the ground floor with its huge dining table is the focus of the house. taking up an entire wall and dominating the space is a vast fireplace, rescued from an old chateau by Mario who decided to make it the centre-piece of their new home.

The couple love music and any guest with a guitar over the shoulder or a penny whistle in the pocket will be cajoled, teased and eventually persuaded to play after supper. The house liqueur generously poured, feet tapping, and recent strangers now firm friends making music together; so many an autumnal evening has been deftly turned into an occasion in the afterglow of a good home-cooked meal *entre amis.*

Florac

Les Tables de la Fontaine
Chambres d'hôtes & restaurant
31 rue du Thérond, 48400 Florac
04 66 65 21 73; 09 66 41 81 12
denis.dessaint@orange.fr; www.tables-de-la-fontaine.com
Restaurant closed Wednesday (and often Thu/Fri lunch off-season)
R: €€
With apologies to a close contender in Langogne, this name is my favourite literary pun on the entire trail. From the outside, the old house looks satisfactorily vintage fairy tale, but just as the restaurant within surprises with its almost stark white walls and restrained modern décor, so the four guest rooms eschew anticipated chintz in favour of clean smart comforts. TV in each room and free wifi connection for guests. Down in the dining room, colour is provided on the plate with proof that Florac owes its allegiance to the more latin counties to the south of Lozère than the montagnard influences of the north. Tapenade, mango chutney and heady Frontignan marinades tickle passion from country produce ranging from foie gras to trout to duck. As popular with the locals as with visitors. Menus from one to four courses on offer.

St-Julien d'Arpaon

Les Trois Tilleuls **
Chambres and table d'hôtes
Domaine des Trois Tilleuls, 48400 St-Julien d'Arpaon
04 66 45 25 54; 04 66 45 25 94; Fax: 04 66 45 25 95
info@les3tilleuls.com; www.les3tilleuls.com
R: €€€ HB: €€€

By the ruins of an old chateau, sink into a pleasant stupor under those equally venerable lime trees that give the house its name and take time to relax after a long day on the road. Spoilt for choice when it comes to accommodation since, as well as the guest rooms in the main B&B, a run of five terraced and semi-detatched cottages are rented out as self-catering gîtes, and marquees in the garden provide budget shelter for hikers. A traditional farmhouse meal with coffee and wine included is the table d'hote option, or a picnic basket can be taken with you for the next day's trek. A laundry room is available to all guests, so a useful point in your travels for refreshing those old socks and jeans. Modest supplement for donkeys.

Cassagnas

Espace Stevenson
Chambres d'hôtes - gîte d'étape, campsite and restaurant
48400 Cassagnas
04 66 45 20 34
contact@relais-stevenson.fr; www.relais-stevenson.fr
R: €€   HB: €€

The blatantly modernised former railway station at Cassagnas, by the waters of the Mimente, is something of a specialist overnight stopover on the trail. Chambre d'hôte option offers rooms with traditional heavy oak furnishings. Gîte d'étape and camping areas on site. You are likely to meet up with guests from across the complex at the table at mealtimes and may round off the evening at the bar, swapping travellers tales.

Le Mimentois
48400 Cassagnas
04 66 45 27 45
lemimentois@yahoo.fr
R: €€   HB: €€

For guests who book in advance, Stéphanie Schirmer can arrange for a relaxing massage to reset the muscles and sinews to default comfort mode after several days on the hoof. Good sized bedrooms and tranquil gardens to continue the chill-out mood.

Saint Martin de Lansuscle

Château de Cauvel ***
Chambres & table d'hôtes, gîte d'étape
Le Cauvel en Cevennes, 48110 Saint Martin de Lansuscle
04 66 45 92 75; fax: 04 66 45 94 76
lecauvel@lecauvel.com; www.lecauvel.com
R: €€€ HB: €€
Extravagant meals are promised at this rather lovely escape from the main Stevenson route. Donkeys subject to supplement. See page 175.

Saint Etienne Vallée Française

Lancize ***
48330 Saint Etienne Vallée Française
04 66 45 46 01
vacances@lancize.com; www.lancize.com
R: €€
A room only option in a cluster of three holiday homes. Barbecue in the courtyard, swimming pool and super views of the village. Mobility restricted guests welcome.

Mialet

Le Pont des Camisards **
Chambres & table dhôtes
30140 Mialet
04 66 85 00 09
francois.destienne@libertysurf.fr
R: €€
Stay with the d'Estiennes at their typical woodland house in the southern Cevennes. Internet access. Covenient overnight stop if you plan to visit the Musée du Désert. See oage 180.

Self Catering & Gîtes d'Etapes

There are three main options for travellers seeking self catering accommodation in France. One is to rent a traditional gîte – often a cottage or annexe to a the owner's private home, fitted out with bedrooms, private kitchen, bathroom and a living room. Ideal for a family or small group. A modern alternative is a purpose-built holiday home or chalet in a holiday complex. The budget choice is to stay at a gîte d'étape or ramblers' hostel.

At a hostel you pay for the bed, rather than the room, and accommodation may be in either dormitories or shared bedrooms. Communal facilities, such as showers and use of a kitchen are sufficient for preparing for the day ahead, without eating into your finances. Some chambres d'hôtes and hotels have gîte détape annexes. The good news is that many gîtes and gîte d'étape properties on the Stevenson trail will also provide a decent hot meal and can offer a half-board (demi-pension) rate combining a bed and an evening meal at a special price.

REMEMBER: Self-catering establishments in France do not usually provide bedlinen and towels. You may need to bring your own sheets (or sleeping bags) or you should telephone in advance to ask about the cost of hiring linens at each stop.

Symbols

R   Room only
HB   Half board (dinner, bed and breakfast)
☺   under 10 euros
☺ ☺   10-20 euros
☺ ☺ ☺ over 20 euros
€   under 35 euros
€€   35 – 50 euros
€€€   over 50 euros
* -***   Official Gîtes de France or Clévacances rating

 Donkeys welcome

 Dogs welcome

Le Puy en Velay

Gîte d'Etape des Capucins

29 rue des Capucins, 43000 Le Puy en Velay
04 71 04 28 74; mobile: 06 63 09 13 69
contact@le-puy.de; www.le-puy.de
R: ☺ ☺
The hostel alternative to an apartment-hotel run by the same family.

Le Monastier sur Gazeille

Chez Emmanuel Falgon

Gîte d'étape & table d'hôtes
43150 Le Monastier sur Gazeille
04 71 03 84 74
gite.monastier@hotmail.fr; http://gitemonastier.chez-alice.fr
Closed: Oct-Mar
R: ☺ ☺   HB €
10 beds in two rooms, with a library, pool-table and garden.

Gîte d'étape communal

43150 Le Monastier sur Gazeille
04 71 03 82 37
R: ☺ ☺
Smart modern communal bedrooms in a former police station. Shared kitchen, showers and toilets.

Goudet

Gîte d'étape and ferme auberge du Pipet

43150 Goudet
04 71 57 18 05
massebeuf.rocher@wanadoo.fr
Closed: mid-Oct – mid-Mar
R: ☺   HB: €
Sleep in bunks in a farmyard barn and buy organic food from the Massebeuf family farmhouse. Two showers and WCs.

Le Bouchet Saint Nicolas

Gîte d'étape Intercommunal ***
43510 Le Bouchet St Nicolas
04 71 57 32 32; fax: 04 71 57 88 01
contact@ccpcp.fr; www.ccpcp fr
R: ☺ ☺

Newly renovated in 2008, the village gîte d'étape boasts 3 dormitories, each housing 6 guests, and two private rooms. A shared kitchen and common room. Accessible to disabled travellers.

La Retirade ***
Gîte d'étape
Auberge du Couvige, 43510 Le Bouchet Saint Nicolas
04 71 57 32 32
jean-paul.pastural@wanadoo.fr
Closed: Feb
R: ☺ ☺   HB: €

At the Auberge du Couvige, you will be able to dine on honest home-cooked country food of the Velay: patés and terrines, creamed puy lentils and fresh fruit tarts. This is the auberge's 23 bed hostel in the centre of Le Bouchet Saint Nicolas. Basic groceries for sale, and whilst there not too much in the way of local shopping if you plan to stock up on food for the journey, your hosts Jean-Paul and Andrée Pastural can tip you off as to which tradesman's van, be it butcher, fishmonger or market gardener, will be tooting its horn on the day of your stay, and they can also rustle up a picnic to take with you. Internet access and cash point.

Landos

Les Fonds
Gîte d'étape
Mairie, 43340 Landos
04 71 08 29 93
lesfonds@wanadoo.fr
R: ☺ ☺

Ground floor accommodation in the centre of the village. Seven rooms for hikers, sleeping 4-7 guests. Dining option only for parties of at least 15 guests. Practical choice for disabled travellers.

Pradelles

Gîte d'étape, brasserie
43420 Pradelles
04 71 00 87 88
brasseriedumusee@orange.fr
R: ☺ ☺   HB: €€
A ramblers' hostel next to the village brasserie in the picturesque village of
Pradelles. Before leaving, check out the church and the museum of
working horses – to inspire your own donkey to greater things.

Les Anes à Gilles
Yurts
Les Ecuries du Musée , Rocher de Grelet, 43420 Pradelles
04 66 69 49 35; mobile: 06 81 60 76 58
gilles.romand@wanadoo.fr; www.lesanesagilles.com
Closed: mid-Sep – mid-May
R: ☺
Mongolian Yurts in the Stevenson heartland. Camping and self-catering
with a difference. See page 157

Langogne

Cap Défi
Self-catering gîte apartments
48300 Naussac
04 66 46 66 46
infos@cap-defi.com; www.cap-defi.com
R: (gîte for 4 people) €€€
Take a few days away from the RLS itinerary and create your own
adventures on and off the water. Not on the Stevenson list, Cap Défi is a
watersports complex on the edge of the man-made lake of Naussac. Down
by the jetty is a bar-café and the front desk for booking a sporting treat,
sailing, canoeing or mountain biking. On the upper level are suites of self-
contained holiday flats, all well equipped and many boasting superb views
across the lake. Two of the apartments have been superbly designed for
wheelchair users – and more adapted flats are planned in the future. Youri
Baillou, the enthusiastic organiser of the sports complex has a zealous
approach to accessibility. Not only are the apartments so well adapted that
wheelchair users can get right up close to the cooker in the kitchen and

practically perform wheelies in the bathroom, but plans are laid to adapt sailing boats and catamarans on the lake for disabled sportsmen and women. An all-terrain wheelchair for rent opens up woodland trails to all and more adapted watersports facilities are on the cards. Great family-friendly accommodation, for short breaks or full weeks.

Cheylard l'Évêque

Le Refuge du Moure
Gîte d'étape
48300 Cheylard l'Évêque
04 66 69 03 21
info@lozere-gite.com; www.lozere-gite.com
Closed: Nov-Mar; first week in July
R: ☺ ☺   HB: €€
The hostel option at the lovely guesthouse with is delicious food options. See review page 167.

Saint Laurent les Bains

Abbaye Notre Dame des Neiges
Maison de Zachée, 07590 Saint Laurent les Bains
04 66 46 59 13 or 04 66 46 59 02 (Mon, Thu, Fri 10-12);
fax: 04 66 46 33 06
maisondezachee@notredamedesneiges.com; www.ndneiges.free.fr
Closed: Nov – Easter
Probably the closest you'll get to the spirit of Stevenson's original travels is to overnight, like the author, in a monastery. The 19th-century monks provided some of the most memorable interludes in the original saga, and at the ice-white abbey of Our Lady of the Snows, the monastic tradition of hospitality to wayfarers continues to this day.

We digressed from days in Lozère across the departmental and regional border into the chestnut country of Ardèche, and the driveway to the abbey along a long shady lane o'er-vaulted by age-old trees. The land around the imposing abbey buildings was once farmed and tended by the monks, who until recently even made their own wines. Although the wines are now produced elsewhere, an interesting range, with food and crafts from other monasteries in France may be discovered in the abbey shop.

Our Lady of the Snows

These days, fewer than 20 monks live at Notre Dame des Neiges, where Stevenson stayed for 3 nights, and their routine is punctuated by the timetable of services, so do make sure that you telephone at an appropriate time when reserving your stay. Book at least 15 days in advance of your visit. The abbey can accommodate up to 22 guests and has 14 pleasantly furnished bedrooms at its Maison de Zachée. Bedspreads are provided, but you should bring your own sleeping bag or bedding. Trappist Cistercian monks do not charge for accommodation, but visitors should give a donation each according to his means, and guests are expected to lend a hand with the chores (perhaps sweeping or washing up) before setting off on their way. There are no visitors' tours of the abbey, which is still essentially a place of prayer and study, but a film show, telling the history and life of the monastery is screened on site. Simply ask on arrival.

La Bastide-Puylaurent

L'Etoile
Chambres & tables d'hôte and gîte d'étape
route de Mende, 48250 La Bastide-Puylaurent
04 66 46 05 52
papadimitriou4@hotmail.com; www.etoile.fr
Closed mid-May – mid-Sep
HB: €€
Half-board conviviality. See page 136.

Chasseradès

Le Mirandol **
Hameau du Mirandol, 48250 Chasseradès
04 66 46 01 14
info@hotel-des-sources.fr; www.hotel-des-sources.fr
Closed: Oct-Mar
R: ☺ ☺   HB: €

This is a chocolate box scene just waiting to be painted: old stones and tumbling geraniums nestling in the crook of a brook surmounted by a lattice of tiered bridges, from a step across the water to the giraffe stilts of the Mirandol viaduct built by those same sharp-witted railway engineers that had so entertained Robert Louis Stevenson that night in Chasseradès. Just as the modern viaduc de Millau seems to enhance and celebrate nature on the motorway south of Lozère to the Med, so this 19th century predecessor frames this hamlet washed by the sources of the Allier,

Chassezac and Lot rivers. Monsieur Chaptal, mayor of the village, oversaw the conversion of the little farmhouse into a well equipped gîte d'étape, with a good sized kitchen and common room and accommodation for 16 guests welcomed by Madame. The ground floor has been thoughtfully designed, with disabled travellers in mind. Once the steep and slightly rugged path to the front door has been negotiated, a bedroom has been laid out for wheelchair users, with a well considered bathroom. If you prefer not to cook, is served at neighbouring Chasseradès, where the family's Hotel des Sources provides good country eating – see page 168.

Le Bleymard

Les Alpiers

Gîte d'étape
48190, Le Bleymard
04 66 48 67 19
pedibuslozere@wanadoo.fr; www.randonnee-lozere.com
Closed Nov-Mar
HB: €€
See page 137 for more on the ramblers lodge hosted by Madame Abenque. Accommodation for disabled guests available.

La Combette

Gîtes
48190 St. Jean du Bleymard
04 66 48 61 35; fax : 04 66 48 61 36
lacombette@wanadoo.fr; www.lacombette.com; cevennes-mont-lozere.com
R: €€   HB: €€€
Holiday chalets and a larger family gîte. One chalet is fully accessible to wheelchair users. The site includes chambres and tables d'hôte and internet access is available onsite.

L'Escoutal
Gîte d'étape
Hameau du Bonnetès, 48190 Le Bleymard
Tél. : 04 66 48 64 08; mobile 06 78 27 12 97
nathalie.bocquee@hotmail.fr; www.gr70.com/bleymard.htm
R: ☺ ☺   HB: €
The budget overnight option at the Bonnetès hamlet. See page 138.

Mont Lozère Ski Resort

Le Montlo

48190 Mas d'Orcières, Station du Mont Lozère
04 66 45 81 30
info@lemontlo.com; http://www.montlo.com
R: ☺ ☺   HB: €
Indoor and outdoor sports catered for, and rooms sleeping up to 10 guests.

Le Refuge

Gîte d'Etape
48190 Mas d'Orcières, Station du Mont Lozère
04 66 48 62 83
guylene.frouin@orange.fr; http://vacances-cevennes-lozere.com
Closed: Nov
R: ☺ ☺   HB: €
Stopover at the ski resort, rent winter sports equipment or hang out at the bar of the on-site hotel. Disabled access.

Le Pont de Montvert

Gîtes du Chastel **
48220 Le Pont de Montvert
04 66 45 84 93; mobile: 06 80 21 14 10
gites-lozere@cevennes-gites.com; www.cevennes-gites.com
R: ☺ ☺   HB: €€
A cluster of little vine-draped houses above the skittish waters of the Tarn and a hefty Camisard's stone's throw from the famous bridge – this is a decent self-catering option with several of the houses boasting their own wood-burning fires for toasting aching tootsies after a week on the trail. Sleeping up to 8 people across two bedrooms and a mezzanine, they are a comfy size for a couple or practical for a family of 4-6, with a proper bathtub, a well-equipped corner kitchen boasting even a dishwasher, a washing machine and a living area with TV and DVD, and even a barbecue outside on the private terrace. This is the countryside, so no 24-hour reception desk. If your hosts are not at home when you arrive, just let yourself in (there will be a note addressed to you on the door, with a key on the table). Make yourself at home and Jean-Marc Brunel will pop round to welcome you later on. One tip: Jean-Marc prefers guests to call on the

landline when booking (and especially if cancelling or changing a reservation) as mobile signals can be a little dodgy in the mountains.

Gîte d'Etape & Camping Communaux **
Mairie, 48220 Le Pont de Montvert
04 66 45 80 10
mairie.pont.de.montvert@wanadoo.fr
R: ☺ ☺

Next door to the Musée du Mont Lozère is a big new municipal gîte d'étape and campsite. Right by the waterside, so if you fancy slipping your shoes off and taking the plunge, the river Tarn is far more refreshing than any namby pamby power shower!

Florac

Val Village des Vacances (VVF)
Pont de Tarn, 48400 Florac
04 66 45 01 21
florac@valvvf.fr; www.causses-cevennes.com/VVF-villages-florac/
Closed Oct – Mar
R: ☺ ☺

A purpose-built holiday village in the national park, and usually packed with families at the height of the season, makes for a practical base for touring the Stevenson sites in the off-peak months. The simple bungalows are holiday-home standard and range from a modest studio with two bunks to a family chalet sleeping six. Three units are fully adapted for wheelchair users. A laundry room is also available. Prices higher in peak season.

La Carline - Le Presbytère
Gîte d'étape
16 rue de Pêcher, 48400 Florac
04 66 45 24 54
lagrave.alain@wanadoo.fr
Closed: Nov - mid-Mar
R: ☺ ☺

On the main street leading to the market place the big wooden door of this 300 year-old presbytery opens to a ramblers' hostel with 18 beds.

151

Chez Proust in Florac on market day

A garden area on the upstairs terrace of the hostel is great for chilling out on a summer's evening, and the cafe Chez Proust up the road is the perfect spot for people watching when the farmers and market gardeners from the surrounding villages come to town to sell their wares on a Thursday morning.

Mijavols

Gîte d'étape & table d'hôtes de Mijavols
48400 Mijavols
04 66 45 09 04
R: ☺ ☺   HB: €

Slap in the middle of a photo opportunity is the hamlet of Mijavols. A simple hostel sleeping up to 20 travellers with a table d'hôte dinner option when you know you'll never make the market town distractions of Florac before nightfall. Modest supplement for donkeys.

Saint Martin de Lansuscle

Malafosse
Gîte d'étape & table d'hôtes
48110 Saint Martin de Lansuscle
04 66 45 75 80; 04 66 45 95 65
malafosse@free.fr; www.causses-cevennes.com/malafosse/bed-and-breakfast.htm
R: ☺ ☺   HB: €

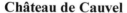

A couple of kilometres from the GR70 as you travel south, a traditional stone Cévenol mas with its pale blue shutters offers 19 beds in 5 rooms for travellers making the extra trek for superb autumnal views across the valleys. If you've gathered chestnuts on the trail, then roast them over the open fire in the living room of the gîte. An extra euro may be added to the modest bed price for heating on chilly nights, and guests are always welcome to use the kitchen to cook for themselves. However, Jean-Paul and Ginette can prepare an evening meal, should you ask in advance, and are happy to make up a picnic for the next day.

Château de Cauvel
Gîte d'étape
Le Cauvel en Cevennes, 48110 Saint Martin de Lansuscle
04 66 45 92 75; fax: 04 66 45 94 76
lecauvel@lecauvel.com; www.lecauvel.com
R: €€   HB: €€ - €€€

This family-run chambre and table d'hôte hideaway from the trail has a gîte d'étape option. Modest supplement for donkeys. See page 175.

Saint Germain de Calberte

Le Recantou

Gîte d'étape and snack bar
48370 Saint Germain de Calberte
04 66 45 90 34; mobile: 06 68 40 90 34
R: ☺ ☺   HB: €€
gilles.des-touches@orange.fr; http://causses-cevennes.com/le-recantou.htm
Four gîte d'étape bedrooms each sleeping 2-4 guests. For more than a century, this little eatery and bar has been a popular rendezvous for locals and those passing through Saint Germain. See page 176.

Les Clédelles

Holiday village
48370 Saint Germain de Calberte
04 66 45 92 97
cledelleslacan@wanadoo.fr; www.lescledelles.com
Closed: late-Oct – mid-Mar; mid-Jun - Aug
R: ☺ ☺   HB: €
Saint Germain is at the heart of Camisard country, now a protected national park. Les Clédelles is a cluster of modern holiday homes in traditional stone and timber within a village vacances holiday complex. Swimming pool, tennis courts and equestrian centre. Self-catering villas for groups of up to 4 or 6 from under 100 euros for one night off-peak.

Saint Etienne Vallée Française

La Fregère

Gîte d'étape & table d'hôtes
Le Pont de Burgen, 48330 Saint Etienne Vallée Française
04 66 45 75 30
gites-rando.cevennes@wanadoo.fr; www.gite-randos-cevennes.com/
Closed: mid-Nov – Feb
R: ☺ ☺   HB: €€
This is a treat for hikers with an appetite, for Dominique Donnet and Alain Pigache grow organic food for the table from their own kitchen garden in the hamlet of Le Pont de Burgen on the banks of the river Gardon. Summer guests dine together on the terrace within sound of a stream; once the nights draw in, then a table by the fire serves to nudge fellow travellers to conviviality. Hostel accommodation or family rooms, with use of a

kitchen. Your hosts may rent out donkeys or plot a tailor-made digression from the trail should you wish to linger longer and explore the countryside or local sporting options for a day or two before getting back on course for Saint Jean du Gard.

Camping

The camping option is usually the best value, and certainly the choice most in keeping with Stevenson's own journey. Happily, modern sleeping bags and equipment are less wieldy than the impedimenta of our literary hero. Nonetheless, these days you may not simply pitch a tent by the wayside in France. Always ask permission from the landowner. Camping is strictly forbidden in the National Parks, which effectively rules out most of the southern section of the trail. But wherever you do camp out, remember the country code, close gates and do not light a fire. On the other hand, some official sites and picnic areas have proper barbecues for cooking al fresco.

Campsites may range from a simple field outside a farmhouse to fully equipped commercial venues with electricity, hot and cold running water, even swimming pools and entertainment. You'll often find a laundry area with washing machines (sometimes ironing boards as well) and you may be able to get internet access. Municipal sites are usually maintained to a good standard, often with shower and toilet facilities designed for disabled users. An onsite shop may provide basic foods, but check whether a campsite is close to village shops or has a daily bread delivery in order for a decent breakfast before hitting the road. Farm sites and fields near chambre and table d'hôte establishments are most likely to have good produce for sale. Caravan and motor-home places are limited, so booking is advisable.

Sometimes you will find an unexpected bonus, such as the chance to camp out in a Mongolian yurt by the donkey stables at Pradelles, or an evening watching beavers building dams on the Tarn at Bédouès. Several sites will rent out a caravan if you are travelling without your own shelter. And of course, at most sites, you'll be able to bring your donkey (check listings for details).

Three quarters of the trail is well served by camp sites. But, since there are very few opportunities to pitch a tent once you pass Florac, consider gîtes d'étapes or holiday park chalets as budget alternatives to hotels and guesthouses on the southern section of the trail.

"Campings", as the official franglais term has it, are usually well signposted, but rarely have a street address. So if you get lost, go to the mairie, the tourist office or ask at any shop.

Symbols

R   Room only
HB   Half board (dinner, bed and breakfast)
☺   under 10 euros
☺ ☺   10-20 euros
☺ ☺ ☺ over 20 euros
€   under 35 euros
€€   35 – 50 euros
€€€   over 50 euros
* -***   Official tourist office or "sunflower" rating

Donkeys welcome

Dogs welcome

Le Monastier sur Gazeille

Le Moulin de Savin
43150 Le Monastier sur Gazeille
04 71 03 82 24; or the Mairie on 04 71 03 80 01
Closed: mid-Sep-May
☺
A friendly welcome at the municipal campsite, with the option of breakfast as you start the long journey south. A small shop for last minute essentials and cold drinks. Some facilities for disabled guests.

Pradelles

Les Anes à Gilles
Self-catering yurts
Ecuries du Musée, Rocher de Grelet, 43420 Pradelles
04 66 69 49 35; mobile: 06 81 60 76 58
gilles.romand@wanadoo.fr; www.lesanesagilles.com
Closed: mid-Sep – mid-May
☺   HB: €
Stevenson pioneered the concept of the sleeping bag when he made his journey through the heartland. You could capture the spirit of eccentricity

and bring a touch of the exotic to your own stay by overnighting in a mongolian yurt. Overnight in a yurt chez Gilles Romand, a favourite and veteran provider of donkeys to Stevenson pilgrims (see page 119). Up to four people may share a yurt, with cooking facilities, shower wc etc on site. This is the environmentally responsible option with solar and wind-powered electricity on site. Pick up useful books and maps for the donkey trail here, including lovely postcards illustrating the various stages of the route, pictures of Gilles' donkeys and Marie-Noelle Lapouge's delightfully illustrated children's book "Les Aventures de Modestine" retelling the journey from the donkey's perspective.

Langogne

Camping Le Lac de Naussac
48300 Langogne
04 66 69 29 62
info@naussac.com
www.naussac.com
Chalet for 4: €€€
Campsite by the lakeside. Wifi, bar and meals - see page XXX

Luc

Les Galets
c/o Mairie, 48250 Luc
04 66 46 60 07
mairie.luc48@wanadoo.fr
Closed Oct-Apr
☺
Campsite beside the river Allier. Shower block.

La Bastide – Puylaurent

Camping de l'Allier **
Route de Mende, 48250 La Bastide - Puylaurent
04 66 46 04 06
campingdelallier@wanadoo.fr; http://campingdelallier.monsite.orange.fr
Closed: late-Oct – mid-Apr
☺

Pitch your tent or rent a mobile home here. Laundry area, TV room, bar and snacks. Canoe and mountain-bike hire. Some facilities for disabled guests. Less than 2km to La Bastide for bakery, butcher, pharmacy and doctor.

Chasseradès

Aire naturelle de camping **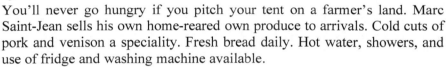
Ferme Prat-Claux, 48250 Chasseradès
04 66 46 06 64; mobile: 06 73 04 14 08
Closed: Nov-Apr
☺
You'll never go hungry if you pitch your tent on a farmer's land. Marc Saint-Jean sells his own home-reared own produce to arrivals. Cold cuts of pork and venison a speciality. Fresh bread daily. Hot water, showers, and use of fridge and washing machine available.

Le Bleymard

La Gazelle *
48190 Le Bleymard
04 66 48 60 48
mairie.du.bleymard@wanadoo.fr
Closed: Nov-Apr
☺
Municipal campsite under shady trees by the banks of the Lot. Lives up to the homonym of the village, as a place for the happy-go-lucky. Some facilities for disabled guests.

Le Pont de Montvert / Finiels

La Barrette ***
Hameau de Finiels, 48220 Le Pont de Montvert
04 66 45 81 82 or 04 66 45 82 16
www.gites-mont-lozere.com
☺

Granite rocks dot this gently sloping little campsite attached to a family home. Pitch your tent or park your caravan and enjoy the views. A smart stone barbecue, and usual facilities (showers, wcs, washing machine, freezer etc) available. Small supplement for donkeys.

Camping Communal **
Mairie, 48220 Le Pont de Montvert
04 66 45 80 10
mairie.pont.de.montvert@wanadoo.fr

☺
Beside the gîte d'étape at the museum of Mont Lozère. See page 156.

Bédouès

Chantemerle **
La Ponteze, 48400 Bédouès
04 66 45 19 66 (in season) or 04 95 35 33 94 (out of
season); mobile: 06 73 86 53 16
chante-merle@wanadoo.fr; www.campingchantemerle.fr
Closed: Oct – mid-Apr

☺ - ☺ ☺
In Chapter 13, Robert Louis Stevenson describes the "new" road from Pont de Montvert to Florac. He compares the site to Killiecrankie back home in Scotland; "A deep turning gully in the hills, with the Tarn making a wonderful hoarse uproar far below, and craggy summits standing in the sunshine high above. A thin fringe of ash-trees ran about the hill-tops, like ivy on a ruin; but on the lower slopes, and far up every glen, the Spanish chestnut-trees stood each four-square to heaven under its tented foliage."

Barbara Chevallier likes to remind guests of that passage in the story, which perfectly describes the setting of her campsite. Genuinely close to nature (as are so many of the stops on this journey), tiptoe close to the water's edge at sunset. During the day, children of holidaymakers may splash by the river's beach, but in the evening a colony of beavers come out from their lodges in the river bank to work and play.

Tent pitches are spaced well apart from each other, so there is space for mere humans to wallow in nature. The ruins of an old stone sheep pen have been converted into a little snack bar, where panini, salad, chips, pizza and even a breakfast option are available for guests to chilled out to cook.

Bring your own wine to raise a grown-up glass to the rising moon once the kids are tucked up in their sleeping bags. Bread and croissants may be delivered to the site on request, and an on-site PC provide a link between timelessness an the unforgiving present. Hot showers and the usual facilities. One shower unit and a wc designed to accommodate wheelchair users.

Le Chon du Tarn **

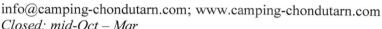

48400 Bédouès
04 66 45 09 14
info@camping-chondutarn.com; www.camping-chondutarn.com
Closed: mid-Oct – Mar
☺

100 pitches and space for few caravans at a charming and well maintained site by the tarn. An age-old orchard provides plenty of shade in summer and a little shop stocks last-minute basics, ice creams, hot drinks and bread. Rent a fully equipped caravan or set up your own shelter. Shower and toilet block. A wifi hotspot and laundry area cater for out-of-tent necessities. Modest supplement for donkeys – but no animal feed available. Facilities for disabled visitors.

Florac

Le Pont du Tarn **

route du Pont de Montvert, 48400 Florac
04 66 45 18 26
contact@camping-florac.com; www.camping-florac.com
Closed Nov – Mar
☺

Mini-golf, swimming pool and plenty of games for children (even twice weekly entertainment during the school summer hols), the campsite, just a kilometre from the market town itself, has direct access to the beaches of the Tarn. On site, the Kaïfi snack bar serves grills and roast chicken as well as daily specials. Pick up fresh bread and croissants daily, catch up on your emails and photocopying, do the washing and ironing and have a quick fix of the 21st century before setting back on the trail to a simpler age. Supplement for donkeys. Facilities for disabled guests.

Dining

Hikers have their GR70 maps, and those strange coloured slashes of paint on trees and telegraph poles to set them in the right direction; motorists have the sat nav sextant in the sky - GPS, that suction caped Polaris of the windscreen - to chart each course; Stevenson had the view at dusk to inspire his course for the morrow. Most of us have an appetite to help interrupt our itineraries.

Whilst you might expect better wine than was served to a nineteenth century Scots traveller, rambling through the long shadows of his phyloxera blighted era, on your plates at farmhouses, inns and many a table d'hôte, you'll find the same sturdy and savoury sustenance that has cheered visitors through the ages .

Entering a village or small town at midday, you might do well to ignore this book and any other serious food guide stashed in Modestine's panniers. Instead, take a leaf out of Stevenson's diary and follow the local form. Many a time and oft have I cast my well laid gastronomic plans to the prevailing winds, and disregarded the most finely starched and perched napkin, well polished wine glass and penmanship of a shrewdly-crafted menu. Instead, I have counted boots. Working boots caked with the very terroir of rural France.

Wherever the heartiest appetites may lead, fuelled by the clean air of the hills, woods, fields and plateaux, the visitor should trust and follow. Perhaps an unassuming café, a tired looking bar with a hundred keyrings and scores of faded bank notes tacked to an old beam above the till, maybe even a garish pizzeria. This is where substantial lunch will be served to even more substantial farm labourers and woodsmen.

Don't expect to dine à la carte, don't ask for a menu. Accept instead the local fare placed in front of you. Perhaps a coarse terrine and salad to start with or maybe a wholesome soup ripe with the DNA of a great grandmother's wisdom never written down. The main course could be the cholesterol path to heaven that is a perfect aligot, or a mutton stew soul-deep in terroir and fleshed with the flavour of the hills. Perhaps, in season, the coveted gigot of young local lamb. The bread basket will be refilled if there is a cheese course, and the meal rounded off with home-made tart or pie.

You won't be offered a wine list, just asked to choose a colour then left to pour liberally from the unlabelled bottle dropped off at the table by the motherly waitress who flirts with the locals sharing your table, calls a sharp reminder to the kitchen and offers a promise, over her shoulder, that she will be right with you.

REMEMBER: Whilst dining rooms in hotel restaurants are usually open to non-residents, many gîte, chambre d'hôte or table d'hôte establishments may only serve meals to guests staying overnight. So do call to check. It is worth reserving whenever possible as, even out of season, restaurants are often fully booked – and in the heart of the Cevennes countryside, you may be several miles or more from the next folded napkin!

Symbols

HB   Half board (dinner, bed and breakfast)
☺   Menus start at under 20 euros
☺ ☺   Menus start at 20-30 euros
☺ ☺ ☺ Menus start at over 30 euros
        REMEMBER: These are only starting prices – a la carte or alternative menus on offer may be more expensive!
        HALF BOARD RATES for many establishments may be found in Accommodation listings.

* -***   Official tourist office rating

Donkeys welcome

Dogs welcome

Le Monastier sur Gazeille

Le Provence
avenue des Ecoles, 43150 Le Monastier sur Gazeille
04 71 03 82 37; 04 71 08 36 88
leprovence.lemonastier@wanadoo.frnture; www.le-provence.com
☺

If you want to start the journey nice and early, first thing in the morning, then check into an hotel at Le Monastier the night before you start out. The

Provence has simple smart rooms with TV and shower and the familiar wooden beam and check tablecloth type dining room for a good old fashioned meal with decent portions of locally sourced food cooked to reliable family recipes within the most modest of budgets.

For well under 20 euros, opt for a menu du terroir to eat generously of the sterling country fare of the Auvergne. Dinners and lunches are stoutly carnivorous, with meats both hot and cold at the heart of every meal (although the celebrated Truite du Lignon is a worthy and honourable alternative during trout fishing season March-August). Expect to find the eponymous puy lentils playing their part in boosting the veal, lamb and guinea fowl for which the Velay is justly renowned, and even if typically verbena-liqueur-infused desserts tempt you otherwise, do not miss out on the cheese course. I've a vested interest in promoting Auvergne's Saint Nectaire (Some years ago, I was officially inducted as a commander of the gastronomic order and presented with a handshake, air-kiss and huge round ripe farmhouse cheese – which unofficially guaranteed me a train carriage to myself when I carried it home in a heatwave), but at Le Provence, I would certainly nod you towards the chabrirou goats cheese as well.

Alain Vincent is the second generation of his family to run the hotel, and he is an enthusiastic supporter of the Stevenson trail. He can also take bookings for the gîte d'étape hostel accommodation on rue Saint-Jean for more budget conscious travellers, and where a bed costs a fraction of the hotel's room rate.

Auberge des Acacias ☺ See page 125.
Chez Emmanuel Falgon ☺ See page 143.

Goudet

La Loire ☺ ☺ ☺ See page 126.
Gîte d'étape et ferme auberge du Pipet ☺ See page 143.

Le Bouchet Saint Nicolas

Chez Andrée et Augustin ☺ See page 135.
L'Arrestadou ☺ See page 134.
Auberge du Couvige ☺ See La Retirade page 144.

Pradelles

Brasserie ☺
The village brasserie next to a gîte d'étape. See page 145.

Langogne

Le Modest'inn ☺ ☺ See page 135.
Les Terrasses du Lac ☺ See page 127.
Le Grill du Gaillard ☺ See page 127.

Domaine de Barres
Route de Mende, 48300 Langogne
04 66 46 08 37; fax: 04 66 46 23 42
domainedebarres@yahoo.fr: www.domainedebarres.com
☺ (lunch only) - ☺ ☺
Of course it is cheating, a smart modern golf club serving a business-class luncheon-lite is hardly in the spirit of the young Stevenson sharing bread with donkeys, monks and itinerant engineers. But remind yourself that yon Robbie was a Scot first and foremost, and you'll not be finding it too off-message to spend time at what is after all a golf club. By the time that you have rationalised that essential truth that Modestine was following in a fine tradition of caddie to the laddie, you'll have banished guilt to the far side of the mountains. The Domaine does boast its golf course within the 65-acre park of tall trees and well maintained lawns. Windows in the wall separating the garden from the grounds offer tantalising glimpses from the terrace of the hotel's club house restaurant.

This is a traditional 18th century gentleman's estate, the old stone building renovated and contemporised with excellent taste by architect Jean-Michel Wilmotte, whose de rigueur obeisance to the cult of glass as the ultimate construction material of the present age is, unlike some of his anglo-saxon contempories, tempered with respect and sensitivity to tradition and situation. So the glass additions to the original manor house are low key and decently framed with wood. Duly modest and at a step removed from the soothingly restored façade of the old buildings, these woodland wings have a Zen-like subservience and strength and appropriately house the swimming pool and sauna. Subtle blending of the modern with the old allows the same sense of space to continue through the rest of the building. Glazing through the kitchens to lounges and bar let natural light flood the ground floor. Bedrooms have a sharply contemporary feel, smoothed to softness by clever use of wood, tiles and leather. I love the sliding doors to the bathrooms – some of which, whilst not fully adapted to the wheelchair user, are well enough designed to accommodate a modestly restricted mobility. Rooms have modern TV and wifi for passing those late hours when fading light shades the lovely views from the windows.

The recent litany of ownership means that the hotel is currently settling into its newest personality. Tweaking of style and approach will doubtless mark coming seasons, but the modern approach to dining shall surely continue. Roaming à la carte will provide the daring reinterpretation of traditional influences that helps city and cosmopolitan type relax when faced with country life. And if you have not spent the morning hiking up an appetite, but merely traded up a mule for a motorised buggy over 9 holes, I am sure that the 18 euro "Golfers' Plate" light lunch option on the clubhouse terrace will be the perfect digestive digression. On the Wednesday noon of our passage through Langone the three-courses-on-one-platter ofering featured a balsamicy chevre salad, rabbit served with a bundle of scrummy girolles mushrooms, bound up in a ribbon of courgette, some prettily chopped veg and a fruit salad. No Languedoc wine on the list – unforgiveable – but a superbly satisfying Viognier (crisp Indian summer in a glass) from Ardèche, just over the horizon – contrition served in full.

Cap Défi
48300 Naussac
04 66 46 66 46
infos@cap-defi.com; www.cap-defi.com
☺
Not in the Stevenson pamphlets, this is just a snack bar-cum-café-cum-clubhouse on the lower level of the block of self catering apartments at the watersports activity centre. Youri Baillou pays the same attention to detail at the waterfront as he does to the gîtes. Everything is totally accessible to all, wide doors and a purpose built wc for wheelchair users. In summer sit outside on the terrace by the jetty and watch the sailing on the Lac de Naussac. Grab a snack lunch and plan an afternoon exploring the sporting options by the lake, on and off the water.

Chaudeyrac

Restaurant de France ☺ See page 127.

Cheylard l'Évêque

Le Refuge du Moure

Cheylard l'Évêque, 48300 Langogne
04 66 69 03 21
www.lozere-gite.com

☺

If the aromas from the kitchen don't seduce you as you walk through the front door of this old stone cottage by Stevenson's quirky church, then the interior décor will turn your head for good

The scent in the hall on the afternoon we arrived at Cheylard was an intoxicating and spicy celebration of September pears with cinnamon and cloves, so I was already wooed and won by the time I glimpsed the cosy little dining room which in the country of the Big Bad Wolf was as close to Little Red Riding Hood's grandmother as I will ever get. The food lures in the guests – and no wonder since Antoine Simonet has cooked for ministers and millionaires in a career that has taken him from the Elysee Palace to the grandest of ocean liners and back to this quaint village. Expect fine local traditional cuisine from the truffade, the veal and the wild mushrooms, but with some spices from further afield. So the sage and broom of the nearby hills might give way to Indian tandoori or spices from exotic isles. Desserts harness and harvest the best of the woods beyond the house, wild berries each in their season rounding of every meal in inventive guise.

It is hard to forget that this is not actually a restaurant. The Refuge is table d'hôte serving dinner and breakfast to overnight guests only and of course it is a team effort, Antoine and his protégées in the kitchen well matched by the charming welcome of Agnes Simonet, who will show you to your chambre d'hôte or perhaps a bed in the gîte dormitory. Breakfast in the morning is a buffet of home made jams, breads, muesli and fruits and, since the Refuge does not serve lunch, there is the option of a picnic basket.

La Bastide – Puylaurent

La Grand Halte ☺ See page 128.
Les Genêts ☺ See page 128.
L'Etoile See page 127.

Chasseradès

Les Sources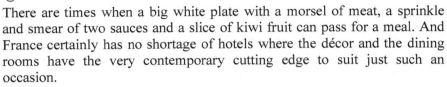
48250 Chasseradès
04 66 46 01 14
info@hotel-des-sources.fr; www.hotel-des-sources.fr
Closed: Nov-Feb
☺

There are times when a big white plate with a morsel of meat, a sprinkle and smear of two sauces and a slice of kiwi fruit can pass for a meal. And France certainly has no shortage of hotels where the décor and the dining rooms have the very contemporary cutting edge to suit just such an occasion.

But frankly, after 15 miles of hiking over hill and dale, as the sun sets over the treetops, 18 inches of glaring white china in a minimalist dining room would not hit the spot. That's why, at under 40 euros for half-board at the Hotel des Sources, a simple one-star hotel room is pretty much perfection at 1200 metres above sea level. Your bedroom may not have the hallmark of the designer, yet it is nonetheless spotlessly clean and basic: if you want to watch telly, go down to the lounge. But what you really need after a day on the Stevenson trail is a good home-cooked meal and no pretentious frills, and in Eric Chaptal's dining room that is exactly what you get.

On the September evening of our stay, a couple of guests grazed à la carte, but most diners were ready for the hearty fare of the demi-pension deal. Our table for two was between a good-natured party of a dozen hikers and several family clusters of four, all in the indoor layers of their outdoor clothes. And each table received the same friendly welcome. Our half-board dinner bed and breakfast stay began with a big tureen of kitchen garden soup on each table. Guests helped themselves to ladle after ladle of comfort food. Slabs of country paté followed, then a third course arrived, this time a steaming crock of quail in a delicious red wine and mushroom jus, with sauté potatos. Two platters of cheese then did the rounds of the room, including one entire wheel of tomme de Lozère. To round off the meal, forest fruits and ice cream. With carafes of table wine and jugs of water and great views of the surrounding hills included in the price, this is a worthy treat with not a lonely sliver of kiwi-fruit in sight. Access to the hotel and restaurant for disabled guests is via the breakfast room at the rear of the building. And there is a family bedroom next to the lounge on the ground floor for those who cannot manage the stairs.

Le Relais de Modestine See page 137.

Le Bleymard

Les Alpiers See page 137.
La Combette ☺ See page 137.
L'Escoutal ☺ See page 138.
La Remise ☺ See page 129.

Mont Lozère Ski Resort

Le Montlo ☺ See page 129.
Le Refuge ☺ See page 130.

Le Pont de Montvert

Auberge des Cévennes
48220 Le Pont de Montvert
04 66 45 80 01
Closed: mid-Nov – mid-Mar

☺   R €   HB: €€

A rarity this one – a chance to wine, dine and sleep at the very inn mentioned in Stevenson's book. At Pont de Montvert "of bloody memory" this is the auberge where our hero was captivated by the bovine sensuality of the waitress Clarisse. A photograph of the sturdy lass herself hangs in the dining room between the windows looking out over the trickly beginnings of the river Tarn. The village stands at the confluence of three valleys, and the old granite inn is perched at an angle to the notorious and eponymous bridge on the opposite bank to the shops and boutiques that lure so many visitors.

On our last visit to Pont de Montvert, we popped into the kitchen of Jean Camus' dining room where the rhythmic satisfactory whack of a cleaver on a fresh consignment of lamb punctuated the conversation. Locally farmed meat and hunters' forest spoils dictate the menu with dishes that the original hiker would have recognised, yet presented here with a deft contemporary touch. Another concession to our age is that it is not just viands that are offered for dispatch "in an intricate sword-play of knives", since the crystal-clear waters beneath yield fine fresh trout for the table.

Clarisse - her memory and her image live on at the Auberge in Pont de Montvert.

Even the classic vegetarian standby will for once elicit genuine yelps of enthusiasm, since the woods that frame every view are thick with wild mushrooms and an omelette aux cèpes is still an occasion on any plate.

It is not merely Clarise's portrait that lends authenticity to the hotel. The dining room seems as the young traveller himself might have recognised it. Stevenson is coy as to his practical and physical reaction to the promise in the batted eyelids of his waitress, but should the wish to linger longer inflame the hearts of his successors, then stay a while. The hotel above the dining room can accommodate 30 guests.

La Truite Enchantée
48220 Le Pont de Montvert
04 66 45 80 03
Closed: mid-Dec – mid-Mar
☺
By the water's edge in the heart of the village, enjoy classic menus de terroir.

Cocurès

La Lozerette
48400 Cocurès
04 66 45 06 04; fax: 04 66 45 12 93
lalozerette@wanadoo.fr; www.lalozerette.com
☺   R: €€€ HB: €€€

This place just gets better and better. One of the first two-star inns to find itself categorised alongside chateaux and manor houses as the Lozère's principal Demeures of Charm, there is nothing two-star about the hospitality here. Remember to book as, the restaurant was packed even on my last visit on a Wednesday night off season. Chalet style rooms, simply, yet daintily decorated, some with little balconies for sitting out under the stars in the cool of the evening air after a long day's tramping from Pont de Montvert. For more conviviality, sit on the porch and look at the hotel garden across the road, or take a book and settle down in the cosy little lounge bar by the reception.

Pierrette Agulhon has gently put her personal stamp on her family's hotel, in the fresh finesses one finds in the décor each new visit, but most of all her personality shines through in the dining room. Her appreciation of good wine is reflected in a delightful wine list. Don't be afraid to ask for advice – she deftly suggested a Chateau Puech-Haut to accompany a main course of veal with girolles mushrooms, rather than our original more cautious selection, words of wisdom that helped turn an evening into something of an occasion. The selection of menus ranges from under 20 to nearly 50 euros, with some pretty gastronomic experiences in the 30's. The mark of a good chef is in simplicity, and when I choose Grand-Mère Julie's panade de morue dorée over the more obvious delights of trout, mackerel or an orange and raspberry magret de canard. What in less skilled hands would have been little more than a fishcake, proved here a positive seduction of flavours and texture in the lightest creamy garlic sauce. Willpower loses its appeal when the cheese board arrives at the next table. That Roquefort, oh gosh, wow. Even the delicious sablé breton et chiboust citron-fraise that followed could never erase the memory of a cheese to make the veins tingle.

Florac

Grand hôtel du Parc ☺ ☺ See page 132.

Adonis
Hotel Gorges du Tarn, 48 rue du Pêcher, 48400 Florac
04 66 45 00 63; fax: 04 66 45 10 56
gorges-du-tarn.adonis@wanadoo.fr; www.hotel-gorgesdutarn.com
Closed Nov-Easter; Wed except Jul-Aug
☺

Calling the restaurant at the Hotel des Gorges de Tarn (see page 132) the Adonis is but a slice of cruelty in an otherwise utopian haven. How on earth could one even hope to attain or maintain the slender silhouette of a god of beauty when faced with the temptations on a menu like this. No, this place should be called Le Chubby Cherub and be done with it, for this is the ideal place to recharge one's embonpoint and consider elasticised waistbands.

Happily, though not on the formal list of suggested stops on the Stevenson trail, this hotel and dining room could not be better placed for walking off a good meal. One of my fellow lunchers stated that she could not eat another thing until evening. I would have been happy to forgo food 'til Friday fortnight, or at the earliest Saint Jean du Gard, 35 miles walk away! I hasten to say it was purely my own lack of will-power that sated me so. Food is not stodgy, but light and lovely. Alas, once I saw how far I could roam for just over 30 euros a head a la carte, the sensible €17 set menu quite slipped my mind!

Two dining rooms suggest different moods, the front room is sharply contemporary in décor, the salon at the back of the hotel, rich in panels and tradition. The kitchen marries both themes with a shrewd reinterpretation of classic ideas and modern concepts. Martial Paulet has some clever ideas in his kitchen and a deft and dextrous way of popping them on a plate. A millefeuille of apple, marinated trout and celeriac, proved a crunch fest to set the meal on the right path, whilst a ravioli of local goats cheese in a chicken stock, and a combination of foie gras orange and gingerbread crumbs wafted interesting aromas across the table. My main course continued the local trout theme and broke the silly rule of white wine with fish, cooked as it was in a fruity red. And as for the dessert of poached pear with three (yes three!) cups of lavender mousse and the eccentric flavouring of a Carambar children's chew sweet, that's my kind of irresponsibility. And, with the range of petits fours that followed, an official farewell to any ambition of an Adonis physique.

Off season, call the hotel and ask to join Martial on one of his Thursday market day cookery classes dedicated to one perfect course – ideal self indulgent digression from the hearty life on the open road. The chef takes his guests to the market and explains how to spot the finest produce, then trots back along the rue des Pêchers to the Adonis kitchens for a lesson in how to make the most of the ingredients. At least two sessions a year concentrate on desserts and other themes include mushroom and game in autumn. The final course looks at the French Christmas dinner, beginning with foie gras...

Chez les Paysans
2 rue Théophile Roussel , 48400 Florac
 04 66 31 22 07
anthony.molloy@orange.fr
☺
This one is a lunchtime gem (although open in the evenings as well). The Maison des Paysans is a co-operative grocery store selling jars, bottles and brown paper packages from farms across the Cevennes. Delicious fruit juices, true kitchen-table pates, preserved fruits and intriguing condiments. Our shopping basket yielded honeys and a terrine flavoured with juniper berries. Next door to the shop is the restaurant, where you may dine on much of the same food, all sourced from farmers the chef will know by name. Eat inside or sit at the front underneath a fruit-laden vine. The clientelle is as eclectic as the menu, with market gardeners, housewives, artists and politicians breaking bread cheek by jowl. Easy wheelchair access from the street.

Le Globe
l'Esplanade, 48400 Florac
04 66 45 00 32
globe.florac@free.fr
☺
Cafe-bar with tables under the shady trees of the main esplanade of Florac. Range of appetite filling options for lunch, but a good tip for a 5 euro breakfast before setting off for a good long walk. Wifi for sifting through the accululated spam of an overlooked inbox.

Les Tables de La Fontaine ☺ See page 139.
Closed Wed (and Thu/Fri lunch off-season)

173

Chez les Paysans

Mijavols

Gîte d'étape et table d'hôtes de Mijavols See page 153.

Cassagnas

Espace Stevenson ☺ See page 140.

St Martin de Lansuscle

Château de Cauvel

Le Cauvel en Cevennes, 48110 Saint Martin de Lansuscle
04 66 45 92 75; fax: 04 66 45 94 76
lecauvel@lecauvel.com; www.lecauvel.com
☺ ☺   R: €€€   HB: €€

This one is still on my to do list. The problem is that Cassagnas is the
penultimate over night stop on Stevenson's original route, and to be honest,
by the time I leave Florac, I've eaten so well that I know I'd never be able
to do justice to Anne-Sylvie Pfister's "decathlon gastronomique" as dinner
is known in these parts.

Madame is known for blending gastronomy with a light touch, but even so,
despite €65 half-board rate for this marathon of meals, I intend to make a
special journey to the chateau just to wallow in a menu that has already
made me consider putting my taste buds on valium. You don't believe me,
well salivate on this October 2008 offering for Stevenson's anniversary:
pear and roquefort mousse, tart aux cêpes (slap bang in season of course),
chevre salad, confit of home reared lamb, cinnamon-infused artichoke
ragoût, chocolate and mint fondant, profiteroles all rounded off with a
spiced citrus soup. And I didn't mention the cold meat and cheese courses.

Although this is a chateau, it is still a chambre d'hôte establishment rather
than an hotel. Perched amid its hamlet, below the chestnut-lined path
where Stevenson heard a woman singing "some old endless ballad about
love and a bal amereux", this is a family home with bedrooms that are
delightfully decorated, elegant and quirky – a bathroom area cordoned off
by a curtain rather than a door, perhaps, or the sloping ceilings of a smartly

converted garret. Tasteful décor within, old stones embraced by clinging greenery without.

As I say, it is a slight detour from the official stop as Cassagnas, but since it is on the GR70, there really is no excuse not to stop off and indulge yourself with virtually every flavour of the Cevennes on a plate. And if you feel that after 11 nights of eating well off the land, the meal might be a daunting task, I make one simple suggestion: do the trail backwards, south to north, you'll then have the best part of a fortnight to walk it all off.

Gîte d'étape et table d'hôtes de Malafosse See page 153.

Saint Germain de Calberte

Le Recantou
Gîte d'étape & snack bar
48370 Saint Germain de Calberte
04 66 45 90 34; mobile: 06 68 40 90 34
gilles.des-touches@orange.fr; http://causses-cevennes.com/le-recantou.htm
☺   R: €   HB: €€
The Touches family's 4 bedroomed gîte d'étape in the centre of the village is very much a meeting place. The little rooms sleep 2-4 people, but the heart of the place is downstairs on the terrace and around the tables in the restaurant. Le Recantou is a bar and eaterie. A snack bar for grabbing a pizza and a beer, a coffee and advice on trout fishing in the tumbling waters nearby, a meeting place for sharing your own travellers tales or listening out for tips from those who know the country well. Walkers have broken their journey here for more than a hundred years. The family have menus going back through generations of country suppers. In 1901, you might have dined on Italian pasta soup and tête de veau and main courses of veal, lamb and chicken cooked to recipes still recognisable today. The meal included lemon tart, fresh fruit and an 1895 wine, with coffee and cognac. These days, you could settle down and linger over the latest incarnation of the menu of the day, or simply knock back a restorative coffee before hitting the trail anew. You might stop here to pick up your emails or just a roast chicken for sharing later on or a jar of locally produced preserves to enliven the baguette for tomorrow's breakfast on the hoof.

Saint Etienne Vallée Française

La Fregère See Page 154.

Un Dimanche à la Campagne
Allée des Tilleuls 48330 - Saint Etienne Vallée Francaise
04 66 45 75 46; mobile: 06 61 35 57 87
☺

Meat grilled over an open fire and a good value set menu chez Didier Philip. Outside conventional mealtimes, drop in for a coffee or glass of wine or an ice cream.

St Jean du Gard

L'Oronge *
103 Grand rue, place de la Révolution, 30270 Saint-Jean-du-Gard
04 66 85 30 34; fax 04 66 85 39 73
oronge@wanadoo.fr; www.loronge.com
☺   R: €€   HB: €€

An oronge is not a mispelt fruit. It is a mushroom. And no ordinary mushroom at that. It is the emperor of mushrooms, the amanita caesarea to give it its appropriate latin name, and often mistaken for a poisonous toadstool, being the edible second cousin to the death cap that did for Claudius and fast-tracked Nero to the top job in Rome. Since the Cevennes positively postulate with funghi, and any drive along much of the Stevenson trail in late summer and autumn is punctuated with countrymen and women emerging from woodland with armloads of girolles, trompettes de la mort, cêpes and all manner of fodder for a forestière aficionado.

So the hotel on the place de la Révolution, at the end of a two-week treck through the magnificent landscape of the Velay and the Gevaudan, Mont Lozère and Cevennes, bears a name redolent of empire – thanks to a not so humble mushroom that is regularly fêted on the menu served in the vaulted stone courtyard.

The land cedes more than mushrooms to the hotel kitchen: chestnuts from the trees that blur the boundaries of three counties are panfried, then tossed into a salad au lard or enrobed with Armagnac cream as a parfait glacé to top and tail many a meal; sweet onions make chutneys for a fish course; honey and almonds tease a sweet and savoury sensation from Languedoc's succulent pelardon goats cheese, and fresh berries in every season inspire mouthwatering desserts. When game is in season, take time to check out the special menus. Since the flora of the Cevennes inspire so many mealtimes, the fauna too should be allowed to play its part.

Jean-Marc Clerc's restaurant is housed within the original 17th century staging post of Saint Jean du Gard. This was, as Stevenson himself put it "a civilised country of stage-coaches." And this very courtyard had been sending travellers onwards towards Alés and the Mediterranean for some 200 years by the time our hero turned his back on Modestine and hauled himself up to the seat by the driver, took to the road lined with olive trees, and being alone with four or five agreeable young men, did not hesitate to yield to his emotion.

Mialet

Le Pont des Camisards ☺ See page 141.

Alès

Les Fleurs
Brocante Brasserie
44 pl Semard, 30100 Alès
04 66 86 00 81
Closed: late-Dec-mid-Jan
☺
Bric-a-brac, antiques or good old junk. The second hand shops around the station in Alès are great browsing grounds for inveterate bargain hunters. Whatever time you arrive at the end of the journey, you may grab a bite and a drink under the plane trees on the terrace of this brocante – brasserie – café. You can leave your bags here if you fancy prowling neighbouring shops, and the bar staff will give you a map of the town. Easily accessible to disabled visitors.

Diversions, Digressions & Detours

In Auvergne
Stevenson spent the best part of a fortnight bemoaning the 19th century Languedoc wines. So take the opportunity to enjoy a proper beer before you leave. The local brew: Vellavia, from Velay barley.

Pradelles
Velorail is a 4-seater land pedalo running along disused railway tracks. The route takes in a couple of tunnels and three viaducts. A 3-hour loop from Pradelles to Landos or 2-hour jaunt from Pradelles to Langogne.
Vélo-Rail La Gare, 43420 Pradelles
04 71 00 87 46 velo-rail@ccpcp.fr; www.velorailsdefrance.com
Closed early-Nov - early Apr

Langogne
RLS looked forward to time by the lake at Bouchet, but he never found the water. Since his day, a brand new reservoir has been created by flooding the old village of Naussac. An enjoyable alternative to a town centre stopover in Langogne, the watersports centre at Cap Défi offers a range of organised sports on and off the water. See page 145.

Florac
No family with a seven year-old could resist this slight detour. At St Laurent de Trèves, actual dinosaur footprints are preserved in limestone and now classified a national monument. An exhibition of prehistoric life can be found in the village church - one in the eye for those declaring the imcompatibility of creationism and evolution. Whilst in the area, treat designated drivers who'll miss vineyard tasting sessions at the end of the trail by visiting the mineral water source at nearby Quezac. If you really like it, you can tour the Perrier plant too when you get to Nîmes!
www.quezac.com; www.perrier.com

Le Pont de Montvert
Museum of local life and natural history.
Ecomusée de Mont Lozère 48220 Le Pont de Montvert
04 66 45 80 73 ecomusee@cevennes-parcnational.fr
Apri- Sep, daily; Oct-Mar, Sat

Saint Jean du Gard
From April to October, take a steam train from the picture book railway station at St Jean, via viaducts and mountain tunnels, to the potters' colony

at Anduze. There, check out exquisite glazing on world famous flowerpots, or take time off to explore the Bambouseraie - an enchanting park with watergardens, treehouses and over 150 varieties of bamboo. www.citev.com; www.bambouseraie.com

Mialet

Superb museum of Camisard and Hugenot family life and religious persecution. Ingenious hiding places and fascinating artefacts and artwork. **Musée du Désert** Le Mas Soubeyran, 30140 Mialet 04 66 85 02 72 http://museedudesert.com *Closed Dec-Feb*

And further afield ...

Meet the Beasts

There is no mystery about the present-day Beasts of Gevaudan. The legendary monster of the region's past, as bloodthirstily recounted by Stevenson on page 24, may be shrouded in legend and rumour, but today around 120 wolves roam a wildlife park, many living as wild, Siberian and Mongolian varieties in pens. Rangers answer questions about the legends and real life. The park was established in 1985 by Gérard Ménatory and its sponsor is former screen siren Brigitte Bardot – perhaps more associated these days with barking than howling. Dogs not allowed in the park (it upsets their distant cousins), but free kennels at the entrance. Park gîtes in the hamlet of Sainte-Lucie for visitors wishing to stay the week. **Les Loups de Gévaudan** 48100 Saint-Léger-de Peyre 04 66 32 09 22 infos@loupsdugevaudan.com; www.loupsdugevaudan.com *closed Jan-early Feb*

Sleigh-Ride with Bison

Bison disappeared from France around 1500 years ago, now a herd of 35 live in 500 acres of forest and moorland. Visit in winter, when you may tour the snow-covered reserve in a sleigh! Horse & cart trips at other times. **Reserve de Bisons d'Europe** 48120 Sainte-Eulalie-en-Margeride 04 66 31 40 40 info@bison-europe.com; www.bisoneurope.com

Gorges du Tarn

At St Enimie take a boat trip along the waters of the Gorges du Tarn and listen to tales of magic and romance from the boatmen and spend the night at the gorgeous Chateau de la Caze hotel by the water (see pages 108-110). www.ot-gorgesdutarn.com; www.chateaudelacaze.com

Useful Contacts

Stevenson Trail

Sur le Chemin de R. L. Stevenson
Bureau des Associations, 48220 Pont de Montvert
04 66 45 86 31
asso.stevenson@libertysurf.fr; www.chemin-stevenson.org
Mon-Fri 8.30-12.30, 1.30-4.30
The absolute essential first point of contact for planning any visit to RLS country is this remarkable organisation uniting all key establishments on the route. The *Association Sur le Chemin de RL Stevenson* has specialised in welcoming visitors since the GR70/Stevenson Trail first appeared on maps. A dedicated team organises a superb programme of events, from commemorative walks, to theatrical events and art and historical exhibitions, and publishes a free annual map and guide to the route (in both English and French) with updated information on every stop from Le Puy to Alès. This may be found either online or at any member establishment on the route. The association can also tailor trips for groups and suggest special literary or specialist diversions for true Stevenson pilgrims. Officially sanctioned events and establishments may be recognised by the logo featuring Stevenson's face. Online shop for books, guides, gifts etc.

Ramblers Associations

National 01 44 89 93 93 www.ffrandonnee.fr;
Gard 04 66 74 08 15 http://pagesperso-orange.fr/cdrp30.rando
Haute-Loire 04 71 04 15 95 http://lacroiseedeschemins.com
Lozère 04 66 47 17 03 cdrp48@worldonline.fr

Tourist Offices

(Outside France)
Maison de la France www.franceguide.com
Maison de la Région Languedoc-Roussillon (UK) 020 7079 33 44
www.maisondelaregionlanguedocroussillon.com

(In France)
Gard 04 66 36 96 30 www.cdt-gard.fr
Haute-Loire 04 71 07 41 54 www.mididelauvergne.com
Lozère 04 66 65 66 00 www.lozere-tourisme.com

(On the Trail)

Alès 04 66 52 32 15 www.ville-ales.fr
La Bastide 04 66 46 12 83 http://villefort-cevennes.com
Le Bleymard 04 66 48 60 48
Florac 04 66 45 01 14 www.mescevennes.com
Langogne 04 66 69 01 38 www.langogne.com
Le Monastier-sue-Gazeille 04 71 08 37 76 www.jeuneloiremezenc.com
Mont-Lozère (*ski resort*) 04 66 48 66 48 www.lemontlozere.com
Parc National des Cevennes 04 66 49 53 01 www.pnc.fr
Pont de Montvert 04 66 45 81 94 www.cevennes-lozere.com
Pradelles 04 71 00 82 65 www.haut-allier.com
Le Puy en Velay 04 71 09 38 41 www.ot-lepuyenvelay.fr
St Etienne Vallée Française 04 66 45 71 61 www.st-etienne-vf.fr
St Germain de Calberte 04 66 45 93 66 www.coeurdescevennes.com
St Jean du Gard 04 66 85 16 28 http://otsi.st.jeandugard.free.fr
St Laurent des Bains 04 66 46 69 94 www.montagne-ardechoise.fr

Emergencies & Health

Main hospitals are in Mende (04 66 49 49 49) and Nîmes (04 66 68 33 44). Smaller hospitals in Florac and Langogne do not offer A&E services. Police can contact out of hours duty doctors and pharmacists. Staff at hotels and chambre d'hôtes will direct guests to medical attention.

General Emergencies (*from EU mobile phones*) 112
Emergency doctor & ambulance 15
Fire brigade 18
Police 17

Pharmacies

Pharmacists offer traditional and alternative medicines – and will examine mushrooms to sort out poisonous from safe varieties. There are pharmacies (look for the green cross) in the following towns on the Stevenson Trail:

Alès	**Langogne**	**Nîmes**
La-Bastide-Puylaurent	**Le Monastier**	**Pradelles**
Florac	**Le-Pont-de-Montvert**	**Le Puy-en-Velay**
		St-Jean-du-Gard

Physiotherapists

There are several pysiotherapist clinics (*kinésithéapeutes*) at:

Alès	**Le Monastier**	**Le Puy-en-Velay**
Florac	**Nîmes**	**St-Jean-du-Gard**
Langogne	**Pradelles**	

RLS on the GR 70

Le Puy-en-Velay

19 km

Arsac-en-Velay

Le Monastier
22 SEPTEMBRE 1878

10 km

St-Martin-de-Fugères

Lac du Bouchet

13 km

Le Bouchet-
St-Nicolas
22 SEPTEMBRE

6 km

Goudet

Landos

13,5 km

Pradelles

5,5 km

Lac de Moissac

Langogne
23 SEPTEMBRE

16 km

24 SEPTEMBRE
Fouzilhac

Chaudeyrac

Luc 25 SEPTEMBRE

Cheylard-l'Évêque

19 km

La Bastide

N.-D. des Neiges
26 SEPTEMBRE

12 km

Chasseradès
27 SEPTEMBRE

Mirandol

Bonnetés

14 km

Les Alpiers

Le Bleymard
28 SEPTEMBRE

5 km

Le Mont Lozère

8 km

Finiels

5 km

Le Pont-de-Montvert
29 SEPTEMBRE

Bédouès Cocurès

28 km

Vialas

Mijavols

Florac
30
SEPTEMBRE

16 km

St-Julien-d'Arpaon

Cassagnas
1ER OCTOBRE

15 km

Malafosse

St-Germain-de-Calberte
2 OCTOBRE

Pont-de-Burgen

20,5 km

St-Étienne-Vallée-Française

Brugairolles

30,5 km

Alès

St-Jean-du-Gard
3 OCTOBRE

Mialet

Sur
le chemin
de Robert Louis
Stevenson

Towns in **Bold**:
Stevenson's
original overnight
stops in 1878

(Other marked
towns are extra
stops on the GR70)

Distances between
flags in kilometres

Map by Patrick Lescure

*© Association Sur le
Chemin de RL Stevenson*

CONTENTS

Travels With a Donkey in The Cevennes
By Robert Louis Stevenson